# Cognitive Behavioral Therapy Workbook:

The Definitive Step-By-Step Guide for Overcoming Depression and Anxiety, Improving Anger Management and Retraining Your Brain in 4 Weeks or Less. CBT Made Simple

Melanie Thielke

Cognitive Behavioral Therapy Workbook

© Copyright 2020 by Melanie Thielke - All rights reserved.

This document is geared towards providing exact and reliable information in regards to the topic and issue covered. The publication is sold with the idea that the publisher is not required to render accounting, officially permitted, or otherwise, qualified services. If advice is necessary, legal or professional, a practiced individual in the profession should be ordered.

- From a Declaration of Principles which was accepted and approved equally by a Committee of the American Bar Association and a Committee of Publishers and Associations.

In no way is it legal to reproduce, duplicate, or transmit any part of this document in either electronic means or in printed format. Recording of this publication is strictly prohibited and any storage of this document is not allowed unless with written permission from the publisher. All rights reserved.

The information provided herein is stated to be truthful and consistent, in that any liability, in terms of inattention or otherwise, by any usage or abuse of any policies, processes, or directions contained within is the solitary and utter responsibility of the recipient reader. Under no circumstances will any legal responsibility or blame be held against the publisher for any reparation, damages, or monetary loss due to the information herein, either directly or indirectly.

Respective authors own all copyrights not held by the publisher.

The information herein is offered for informational purposes solely and is universal as so. The presentation of the information is without a contract or any type of guarantee assurance.

## *Table of Contents*

*Introduction* ............................................................. 5

*Chapter 1. Cognitive Behavioral Therapy* ....................... 8

*Chapter 2. Activate Behavior* ..................................... 12

*Chapter 3. The CBT Experience* .................................. 19

*Chapter 4. How to Identify Negative Thought Patterns* ..................................................................... 25

*Chapter 5. Break Your Negative Thought Patterns* ....... 32

*Chapter 6. How to Identify Your Core Beliefs* ............... 38

*Chapter 7. Change Your Core Beliefs* ........................... 45

*Chapter 8. Eliminate Procrastination and Work through Worry, Fear, and Anxiety* ............................................ 53

*Chapter 9. Practice Mindfulness* ................................. 61

*Chapter 10. Managing Excessive Anger* ....................... 67

*Chapter 11. Make a Change of Yourself* ....................... 74

*Chapter 12. Break Toxic Connections* .......................... 81

*Chapter 13. How to Practice CBT with your Everyday Life* ............................................................................. 88

*Chapter 14. Develop a Positive Mindset* ...................... 95

*Chapter 15. Identify Your Goals* ................................. 103

*Conclusion* .............................................................. 109

# Introduction

CBT was formulated about forty years ago to help treat people suffering from depression. As the years went by, many of the techniques and steps developed in CBT to handle depression have been applied to a broader set of mental and emotional disorders.

CBT has gone on to treat borderline personality disorder, bipolar disorder, anger issues, alcohol, and drug abuse, childhood depression, spousal or marital conflict, insomnia, eating disorders, fear of the dentist, all sorts of social phobias as well as generalized anxiety. That is a long list. It's easy to see why cognitive behavioral therapy has expanded quite a bit because there are a tremendous amount of science and success stories behind it.

The world of psychology and psychiatry has developed on two tracks. There's always been a "talk therapy" component to treating mental, emotional, and personality disorders. However, relatively recently, more and more practitioners have been leaning on hardwired or biological treatments involving a range of chemical compounds.

This all became popular when the popular antidepressant Prozac entered the global mental health scene. At that point, a lot of people thought that depression was just another illness, kind of like the flu. When you have a head cold, you take a pill. When you're depressed, you take medicine.

This led to a massive explosion in prescriptions for anti-anxiety and anti-depression medication. If you study the top ten most-prescribed medicines in the United States, antidepressants and anti-anxiety medicines will always make a list.

This has raised many alarms because these chemicals have a tremendous impact on the patients' brain chemistry. Without proper supervision and with prolonged use, they can have long-term effects on patients' mental functions.

This is why there's been a renewed and intensified interest in more natural approaches to personality, emotional and psychological issues. Cognitive-behavioral therapy can work with antidepressants, anti-anxiety, and other medications.

However, patients would be better off if they used an utterly chemical-free approach. The person often credited as the pioneer of cognitive behavioral therapy is Dr. Aaron T. Beck.

Dr. Beck focused most of his research on the study of depression. In particular, he wanted to see the connection between depression and cognition or the ability of depressed people to perceive their reality. He noticed that there was quite a link between depression and people's cognitive thinking.

Before Dr. Beck, the prevailing idea was that depression happens, and it leads to negative thinking. Dr. Beck reversed the process. He said that if the cognitive state of the individual patient is positive, then depression can be overcome. It can go the other way, rather than assume that if a person is depressed, then it leads to negative thinking, and not many people can do it.

This was a breakthrough because it led to the core premise of cognitive-behavioral therapy, which involves taking control of how you think. It may seem like your depressed mental state is automatic. It may seem like you don't have much control over it. Still, by taking control of your ability to interpret what things mean in your life, you can arrest that negative emotional slide to sadness, melancholy, and, ultimately, depression.

Dr. Aaron T. Beck's pioneering work laid the foundation for cognitive behavioral therapy, which has grown in leaps and bounds and is now applied to a lot of dysfunctions and disorders.

# Chapter 1. Cognitive Behavioral Therapy

Cognitive-behavioral therapy is a technique used by people to change and transform their life. Most of our decisions and achievements are based on our thoughts. Our thoughts influence our behaviors. As such, if we understand our thoughts, we can change them and, consequently, our actions. Cognitive-behavioral therapy has helped people deal with stress, depression, anger, among other mental conditions. Cognitive-behavioral therapy is a technique used by people to change and transform their life.

Most of our decisions and achievements are based on our thoughts. Our thoughts influence our behaviors. As such, if we understand our thoughts, we can change them and, consequently, our actions. Cognitive-behavioral therapy has helped people deal with stress, depression, complicated relationships, grief, panic disorders, generalized anxiety disorders, marital conflicts, dental phobias, post-traumatic stress disorders, eating disorders, insomnia, and a variety of other mental and physical complications.

We will use cognitive behavioral therapy to identify the thoughts that stir disorders such as depression and anxiety, learn how to deal with negative thoughts, and to fight off stress, anger, and depression. Using cognitive behavioral therapy, we will first assess our beliefs; that is, how we interpret the events of our lives, how we behave due to our thoughts, and finally, how we feel.

The most significant advantage of cognitive behavioral therapy is that it is goal-oriented and focuses on specific issues. Secondly, it is convenient, and one must participate fully to get the expected results. Thirdly, it focuses on the daily challenges, thoughts, and behaviors. Another advantage is that you will know what you want to achieve and how you can get there.

Note that cognitive-behavioral therapy focuses on thoughts, feelings, beliefs, and attitudes; therefore, you will be required to face some of the things your mind wants so much to escape. You might have to face your fears, thought gradually.

Things you will be able to identify include:

- The unhelpful thoughts that might lead to psychological problems,
- The unhelpful behaviors that are affecting your life negatively,
- Better thoughts, habits, and beliefs that will add value to your life,
- The new patterns you apply in your life to relieve mental and physical conditions and even help you act better.
- Did you know that most of your problems mostly arise from the meaning you give to events or situations? If you have unhelpful thoughts about yourself, it becomes hard for you to function well under different conditions.
- Cognitive-behavioral therapy will have a positive impact on how you act and feel. It will also equip you with appropriate coping skills and strategies to deal with the challenges.

### Levels of Thoughts in CBT

Cognitive-behavioral therapy recognizes three main types of thoughts, namely, automatic thoughts, assumptions, and beliefs. Cognitive-behavioral therapy explains that our core beliefs are the causes of our premises, which, in turn, initiate our intuitive ideas and, consequently, our emotions.

Core beliefs are the general centralities that we use to assess the standards we set for ourselves, other people, and the world. Our central core beliefs are typically formed at the impressionable stage of life. We use these beliefs to determine what to think about others. In some cases, our opinions are harmful, and they affect our lives negatively. Negative feelings include, "I am unlovable" or "people are not to be trusted. If one believes that he/she is weak, anxiety may kick in. On the other hand, a positive belief, such as "I am a winner," can build one's esteem.

If one has profound negative core beliefs about him/herself, he/she will be prone to anger, depression, anxiety, stress, among other adverse mental conditions. Using CBT, one can identify the negative beliefs that are leading his/her life in a downward spiral and look for alternative ideas to balance them. You will notice that negative feelings have powerful accompanying emotions, and it is hard to shift them even with contradictory evidence.

Underlying assumptions are those beliefs that direct our decisions in different situations. Usually, underlying assumptions arise from personal experiences. For instance, if one was lied to but a spouse, there might be the assumption that every person in that gender is a liar. Another example of underlying assumptions is when one assumes that if he/she allows a person to discover their weaknesses, the person will leave him/her.

Automatic thoughts occur on a day to day basis, and they help us to make sense of our experiences. Automatic thoughts influence our decisions unconsciously. Have you ever yelled at someone and then could not understand what triggered you?

Automatic thoughts are responsible for most of our automatic responses. For instance, a person might do something that angers you, and immediately, you boil over with anger and let that person have a tongue lashing.

Cognitive-behavioral therapy can help you to understand your automatic thoughts. First, after every episode of involuntary reactions, for instance, a moment of an outburst of anger, assess your ideas. What was going through your head at the moment you were angry? Which feelings were making you act like that? You could write your automatic thought down and assess them carefully.

# Chapter 2. Activate Behavior

### Behavioral Activation (BA)

Depressed people often feel weighed down and apathetic. Even small, everyday tasks such as doing the laundry become daunting. Depression drains you of energy, leaving you asking, "What's the point in doing anything?"

As time goes on, you cut more activities from your daily life, which leaves you feeling even more depressed and worthless. Your motivation continues to dive. You start telling yourself things like, "I can't cope with anything," "I'll never get better," and "I don't enjoy anything anymore."

To break out of depression, you need to stop this cycle. The only way to regain control over your life is to deliberately engage in positive activity again, even when you don't want to. This strategy is known as behavioral activation or BA. The first step is to think of the activities you used to enjoy, as outlined in the other exercise.

Exercise: Planning Positive Activities

Make a list of low-key activities you enjoyed before you developed depression. These activities could be as simple as watching a movie at home. Give yourself time to make your list because depression can make it harder to remember things.

Now plan when you can do three of these activities over the coming week. To begin with, 20 minutes is enough. Make a note of each session in your diary. It's just as important as any other commitment, so don't feel guilty about making time for yourself.

Don't expect to feel excited at this stage. Making this list probably felt like a chore. That's normal! The real progress comes when you follow through and keep a record.

Exercise: Pre- and Post-Activity Mood Record

Before you start a planned activity, make a note of your mood. Give yourself a score of 1-10, where a rating of "1" means "very little energy or motivation" and "10" means "very excited and enthusiastic."

When you've finished, write down your score. Any increase, even if it's just one or two points, is a step in the right direction. Sometimes your score might not change at all. If you feel as though nothing is making you feel better, it may even go down. That's OK. It just means you need to change your planned activity, or perhaps try another time again.

Choose activities that move you closer to the person you want to be.

BA is more effective if you choose activities that are in line with your goals and values. For instance, if you want to be more sociable, setting yourself the purpose of chatting with an old friend for 10 minutes on the phone would be an excellent BA goal.

Finally, make sure you are choosing the activities you want to do, not what you think you should be doing. For instance, don't set yourself the goal of cleaning the bathroom or doing the grocery shopping. Sure, these are essential activities, but the point of BA is to help you re-engage with the things you enjoy. You don't have to look forward to it, just do it anyway.

When you try BA, the little voice in your head might tell you unhelpful things like:

- "This won't work. You never enjoy anything."
- "It can't be this simple. It won't make you feel better."
- "It might work for other people, but not for you."

The secret? Try it anyway. What's the worst that could happen? Even if you try an activity for 10 minutes and feel no different, you haven't lost out on anything. You can then try the other day again or work another event. If you feel motivated on some days but not others, you can rest assured that this is entirely normal.

Progress isn't always linear when it comes to recovering from depression. Some days, you'll feel hopeful. Others, you'll feel defeated before you even start. The trick is just to keep going. When you complete your BA exercises, give yourself plenty of praise. You have every right to be proud!

Once you have some evidence that BA works for you, you can challenge these negative thoughts using the cognitive restructuring exercise outlined. Remember: you need to identify unhelpful thinking, look carefully at the evidence for and against it, and then come up with a healthier alternative thought.

### When to Get Support

If you've tried BA exercises several times and they don't seem to be working for you, it may be a sign that you need further support from a therapist or doctor. Please don't think that you've failed. Sometimes, depression doesn't respond to self-help. If you feel very low or have no energy for even brief 10-minute activities, finding a medical professional can help you take the first steps to recovery.

## Depression, Problem-Solving & Empowering Yourself

A little-known but widespread problem in depression is having trouble making decisions. The good news is that you can sharpen your problem-solving skills. Problem-solving isn't always straightforward, and it can feel overwhelming when your mood is low. At the same time, devising solutions and putting them into practice is very empowering.

When you realize that you don't need someone else to rescue you, your self-esteem will grow. This will help you feel good about yourself, which in turn will help lift your mood.

Seven Steps to Problem Solving

### Work out What the Problem is

In some cases, it's obvious. For example, if you know that you need to choose a new school for your child, solving the problem is a matter of evaluating local schools and picking the best option. On the other hand, some issues aren't so easy to pin down. You might know you are unhappy in a specific situation, but the details are a bit fuzzy.

For instance, if you know that you dislike going into work, you'll need to think carefully about the underlying source of the issue. What is it about the environment or the work itself that is making you sad or depressed?

Upon reflection, you may discover that the problem is, "I need to find a new job," or "I need to be more organized so that I can meet all my deadlines, and have a less stressful time at work."

When you've narrowed down the problem, write it in your notebook. Well done! You're off to a good start.

## Brainstorm a List of Potential Solutions

Let your imagination run wild. Put aside half an hour to make a list of every solution you can think of. Don't worry if they seem strange or unlikely. You don't have to show this list to anyone.

Get some outside input. Ask a couple of people you trust to help brainstorm with you. They will probably come up with some ideas you haven't thought of. When you are stuck in a depressed mood, your problem-solving abilities take a hit. It's easy to become locked into a single perspective.

If you have a severe problem or can't rely on anyone close to you to help out, get some advice from a specialist. Depending on your problem, this person could be a counselor, a helpline volunteer, or a religious leader at your place of worship.

For each solution, ask yourself:

- How much time will it take me?
- How much money will it cost me?
- Will I need any outside help? Will it be easy for me to get this kind of help?
- Will I need any special equipment, training, or resources?
- Are there any critical long-term consequences I should think about?

## Choose the Best Solution

If you're lucky, you'll have found a perfect solution. Unfortunately, in most cases, we have to compromise when solving problems. Writing out the pros and cons, as in the step, and talking to others is so important. Knowing that you have given the matter serious thought will make it easier to believe in your judgment.

Remind yourself that no one makes the right choices all the time. However, we can all try our best to work with the information and resources available at the time. Don't fall into the trap of postponing a decision just because you're afraid of getting it wrong.

*Make a Plan*

Having found your solution, you now need to make a roadmap for the way ahead. Your goal is to draw up a step-by-step plan that leaves you feeling empowered rather than overwhelmed. Make each step as specific as possible.

For example, suppose your goal is to sell your house and move to a new town. One of your first steps is to find out how much your property is worth. It would be more helpful to write, "Schedule a valuation within the following seven days," rather than "Find out how much I could get for my house."

*Execute your Plan*

Start with the first step and go from there. Take it slow and steady—even people who aren't depressed need to be patient and encouraging with themselves when solving problems. You might need to break your steps down further. No action is too small as long as it moves you also toward your goal.

Other strategies that might help:

- Planning a small reward for every step you take
- Asking a friend or relative to give you some support
- Working on a stage for just 10 minutes at a time
- Keeping a log of your progress so you can see how far you've come

### Evaluate the Results

You've reached the final stage on your problem-solving journey. You've implemented the solution. Did it work? If not, what could you do the other time differently? Perhaps something unexpected happened, or you didn't get hold of the information you needed. We can all try our best, but there are lots of things that are beyond our control.

Even if things didn't quite work out as you hoped, give yourself lots of praise. You tried something new, and that's something to celebrate. Remind yourself that problem-solving is a skill. Like all skills, it becomes more comfortable with practice.

Summary

- Behavioral Activation (BA) and problem-solving are two practical tools lots of people find helpful in overcoming their depression.
- BA involves identifying activities you used to enjoy and scheduling time in which to do them.
- It's normal to feel resistance when you try BA, but you need

# Chapter 3.   The CBT Experience

For a client, the first session in CBT can work up a lot of emotions, which can be quite overwhelming. For this reason, this has been put together on what to expect of your first CBT experience.

**1. Expect your nerves to fly:**

Whether or not you are already experiencing anxiety, expect to feel on edge, and become increasingly panicky most of the time. These feelings are usually a result of not knowing what to expect from your first experience. Keep in mind that these feelings are normal and do not raise any cause for alarm. So, keep calm; you aren't having an anxiety attack, and your anxiety hasn't worsened.

**2. Expect some degree of emotional exhaustion:**

Both within your sessions and the days following them, you may tend to feel more tired, exhausted, and increasingly sensitive. These feelings are a natural effect of the process. As a matter of fact, CBT sessions considered more challenging and emotional tend to yield the best outcomes in the long term.

**3. Expect to explore the present and future instead of the past:**

It is a standard process in some forms of therapy to spend time exploring the childhood of the client, their past experiences, and relationships with family members. However, in cognitive behavioral therapy, the case is different. The sessions usually revolve around retraining the present thought pattern of the client and identifying new and better ways to help them manage their thoughts and feelings to progress. This experience can be especially relieving to clients who don't want to bring up their pasts or are tired of therapists digging up context clues from yesteryears. Although this approach is necessary, CBT doesn't implement it.

## 4. Expect a rollercoaster ride:

As it is in any other form of therapy, clients have to learn to expect ups and downs in the process. Cognitive-behavioral therapy is not without this characteristic. In some sessions, the client is bound to feel like they are making significant progress, while other courses might leave them feeling not much progress was made. However, regardless of the feeling that accompanied each meeting of the treatment process, learning took place. Although it may not seem that way to the client, every meeting of the whole process is essential and cannot be done without.

## 5. Expect the process to be time-consuming:

Clients should not be naive in thinking that a couple of sessions will completely solve their problems and make them useful as new. CBT doesn't work that way and requires a relatively long period and lots of practice for any significant progress to be made towards solving the client's problem. In a certain sense, the time seems befitting, because for an extended period, the client has used one specific thought pattern, and any change in thinking habits will take time to be thoroughly enforced.

### What to Expect for Treatment?

The first part of the treatment process is entirely devoted to assessment and evaluation. It provides a platform for the client to communicate with the therapist about any challenges they are faced with, or how they would prefer to use the therapy to achieve. To get a grasp of the client's condition or goals, the therapist will make some inquiries from several critical areas of the client's life. According to the assessment process results, the therapist will evaluate their skills and decide whether they are the right fit for the client's case. If the client's case doesn't fit the therapist's capabilities, the latter will make a referral to another therapist better suited to handle the client. Sometimes, by the time the assessment or evaluation session is completed, the therapist and client should have a suitable plan of treatment that outlines the type of interventions that will be implemented in the process. On other occasions, there might be added assessment sessions to create a better course of treatment. Once the client has successfully agreed on a recommended plan of treatment, he or she will know whether or not CBT is the best form of therapy for their condition.

Therapists in cognitive behavioral therapy make their assessments based on the present state of the client. However, they may tend to inquire about the past sometimes. Therapists will usually seek answers from clients to the questions shown below:

- What are the major factors that trigger the problem?
- Does the problem interfere with your life? If yes, how?
- For how long have you been experiencing these problems?
- What is your driving force to seek change, and how motivated are you about the process?
- In what way could your experiences, peers, or family influence your present condition?

Once the evaluation/assessment session has been concluded, the other courses that would ensue would be aimed at tackling the client's problem. These sessions usually involve more collaboration between client and therapist. The reason is that

CBT involves more activities than other types of therapy. The majority of that time is used in the learning and implementation of coping skills.

Each session following the assessment session would be used to solve the client's issues, unlike in standard therapy, where the majority of the time is used to talk about the client's problems. All the sessions in the process typically follow a similar fashion to make sure that time is used judiciously. Every session starts with a brief period dedicated to checking in, accompanied by a period used in the last session and going over any assigned homework. After this period, the client and therapist go-ahead to create a plan for that session. The remaining time is used in trying to achieve the program.

Studies about cognitive-behavioral therapy reveal that the treatment becomes increasingly active, and improvement tends to be faster in clients when homework is integrated into the treatment process. There might be assigned homework for each session to help the client enforce the skills necessary for the client to overcome their condition. In the early periods of the treatment process, homework would often involve keeping tabs on mood swings or recording specific behavioral patterns over a given timeframe, say, a week. Over time, homework could grow to include recognizing and correcting negative thought patterns, or putting into practice a behavior picked up in therapy sessions, like learning to be assertive with friends and family.

This other phase of treatment after the assessment period is the education stage. This stage is what follows in the ensuing sessions after the first one. At this stage, clients are enlightened on the psychodynamics of their problems. That is, how their present and past may be affecting or influencing their present condition. Clients may get to know how the brain is involved in the enforcement of thoughts and behavioral patterns, even in cases where neither one seems productive. Clients would also be brought into the light about the cognitive behavioral therapy model, which they, in collaboration with the therapist, devised for the treatment process.

The latter stages of the treatment process involve the experimentation or implementation of knowledge learned. The treatment process will take a turn towards the cognitive component to help the client decide better-thinking patterns. Afterward, work will begin with the behavioral part involving performing activities to test the client's assumptions, as well as the ability to recognize and learn better behaviors in the present and future.

As the treatment draws to its final stages and all the client's goals have been achieved, it is right to begin turning down the frequency of each therapy session. In other traditional forms of therapy, clients would be required to be in the system continuously for years unending. However, in cognitive behavioral therapy, clients are taught to be therapists to themselves.

In this vein, when the treatment process stretches towards the final parts, the sessions are scheduled less frequently so that clients can depend on themselves more in implementing the skills they have been taught. Doing this makes sure the client has faith in his or her capability to deal with any issue that arises after the treatment process rather than relying on the therapist.

The concluding part of the treatment process will be spent in practicing and maintaining the knowledge learned. Just as thinking and behavioral patterns have been ingrained in clients over the years, it requires lots of time and practice to reshape their actions and thoughts. The reason is that the mind will typically yearn to return to its comfort zone where the behavior and feelings are unchanged, and only persistent practicing can be used to condition it into acting and thinking in a new way.

When clients finally feel comfortable enforcing their knowledge and coping skills, the treatment is now complete, and the sessions terminated. However, it is helpful that clients' sessions from time to time for a professional viewpoint of their progress.

# Chapter 4. How to Identify Negative Thought Patterns

Negative thinking is likely to rob you of the confidence that you have and feel that you cannot stand going before people. The thoughts instill fear in you, and you end up avoiding social gatherings. When you subject your opinions to negative thinking always, it will result in negative emotions. It can end up making you feel bad and can even lead to depression. The thoughts that you have will determine your mood for your entire day. Positive thinking will make you happy, and you will have a good feeling. Finding a way to suppress negative thoughts will be of importance to you. Replace them with positive ones so that they will not torment you. Some of the negative thoughts that come along with social anxiety are:

### Thinking That People as Bad

When you are in a social setting, each person tends to be busy with their issues. You can meet a calm person and begin a friendship if you can build a good rapport. When you have social anxiety, you are likely to avoid people and think that people do not care about you. You may feel that you don't see your importance being there while as you are the one who is avoiding them. When you find yourself in such a situation in a social setting, its time you know that you have to handle your social anxiety. That will make you feel like the people around you do not like you and hate you for no reason.

### Unnecessary Worry

It is obvious to have unnecessary worry when you have social anxiety. Even when you are on time, you are always worried that you will get late. You will portray a bad image for getting there late. When in a family setting, you are worried that your partner will scold you for lateness. You do things in a hurry so that you do not get late even when you have enough time to go to your thoughts. When you have someone else to accompany you, you will make them do things in a rush. You think like they are consuming all the time and they will be your reason for being late. You will even, at times, threaten to leave them if they don't do things quicker than they are already doing.

### Judging Yourself

Judging yourself is the worst thing you will ever go, and that will make you fear. Deciding whether you will find pleas people or not will make you have much social anxiety. You will be nervous when you start thinking about how people are thinking about your physical appearance. Judging how you other people will view you will make your self-esteem go down. The people you are worried about will think you do not look outstanding may not have an interest in how you look, but what you have to deliver. At times, people do not pay attention to the minor details that are making you judge yourself unnecessarily.

### Criticism

Anytime you know that you will intermingle with people, you fear they will criticize you. You do not even have a valid reason why they will criticize you, but you think it is not wise for you to join them. It is a negative thought, and you need to stop thinking in that direction. No one is going to critic you for no reason, and that should not be considered close to you. You will fear to go to social gatherings, and you will deny yourself an opportunity to learn from your fellow partners. Fearing criticism will make you an introvert, which will make you mean that you will miss much when you choose to stay indoors. When you say something and get someone to challenge you, it will help you be more creative. Criticism is not evil, even though people with social anxiety do not like a situation subject to critics. They will avoid such situations at all costs for fear of humiliation.

### Prejudgment

Although it is wise to think about the future, the art of judging tends to be detrimental. In other words, the aspect of prejudging situations tends to be worse, especially when the opposite of the expectations is meant. In most cases, social anxiety disorder tends to cause people to decide the results of a particular situation. It is worth noting that prejudgment is done in regards to the history or rather a forecast of what might happen in the future.

### Blame Transfer

When a society or the peers piles up unnecessary pressure on someone, the chances of missing the mark is quite easy. In other words, one quickly loses focus and misses the point. As a means of evading the shame or rather the punishment, the victims, in most cases, transfer the blame. For instance, if it issues to deal with academics, the victim may start claiming that time wasn't enough to deliberate on all issues. Others may associate their failures with the climatic changes or the lack of favorable conditions for working. There are cases where the victims tend to be genuine and claim diseases as the cause of their failure. However, the art of transferring blames from one point to another tends to be detrimental and shows signs of being irresponsible.

### Procrastination

One of the significant effects of social anxiety is that is causes one to fail in deliberating on duties and transferring them to another day. In other words, procrastination becomes the order of the day. However, it is worth noting that with procrastination, the expectations are never met. The fear, as well as the sensation of being anxious, sets in. In other words, the victim starts feeling as if they are a failure in the collective and loses focus. More time is wasted as they try to recollect themselves up. More fear sets in, and the victim may end up being restless. Improper management of time is the primary cause of procrastination. In other words, the lack of planning causes individuals to keep working over the same issues and forget about others. For instance, scholars may spend more time with the subjects they like and forget about the others. In other words, they may end up forgetting that all the items will be examined in the long run. The sensations bring more fear and restlessness.

### Find Out the Causes of Your Negative Thought Patterns

The other challenge is to identify the sources of your negative thoughts. For instance, if one of your negative thoughts is, I'm ugly, no one likes me! Try to understand the action or event that triggered this thought. Being good at identifying the causes of our negative thoughts calls us to be introspective. Maybe the source of your negative thinking is your childhood abuse. If a close family member told you that you are not beautiful, you might have taken it to heart, and have been since looking for evidence to support your flawed belief. A member of the opposite sex might look at you with a frown – for other reasons, but you will still deduct from their facial expression that they find you ugly.

### Highlight unhelpful thought patterns.

It is one thing having negative thought patterns, and it is another having unhelpful thought patterns. These are also known as core beliefs. The unhelpful thought patterns are ingrained into a person's psyche. Unhelpful thought patterns tend to be divorced from reality. For instance, if you have been telling yourself, "I'm stupid," for long enough, it will cease being just a negative thought and graduate into a core belief. This will lead you to automatically shunning opportunities and people that you consider too smart for you.

### List down the consequences of your negative thoughts.

To be more involved in actively changing your negative thought patterns, you have to identify the consequences that you suffer. For instance, if your negative thought, I'm foolish causes you to detach yourself from your peers or stop you from going for the opportunities that you deserve. Take note of these consequences so that you may increase your resolve to change your situation. At one point, you will have had enough and decide that you want to change. You may also list down past negative experiences and consequences resulting from negative thinking patterns.

### Keep a record of your thoughts.

Using a worksheet, track the number of negative thoughts you experience daily or weekly. Also, note down the ideas that support thought and the ideas that do not support an opinion. For instance, if one of your negative thoughts is, I'm a loser, plans that do not recommend this negative thought include, "I'm a great person," "I have a sharp mind," and "I don't need everyone to like me!" Try to determine the days during which you experience low cases of negative thought patterns and the days when the negativity shoots through the roof.

### Avoid negative language

Create a list of negative words that you use often. For instance, "can't" and "won't" and make a conscious decision of using more balanced words like "sometimes" or "most of the time." When you have a negative way of thinking, it affects even the language you use. But you must make a conscious effort to alter this situation. By developing a style that promotes positivity, you will be sending a message to your brain to challenge its negative thinking patterns.

Explore the connection between your emotions and negative thoughts

Whenever you experience a negative emotion, start by questioning the thought behind it. For instance, if you get anxious or depressed, go back to the feeling that you just had. You will find that the atmosphere was depressive. For example, you might have wondered why you have taken so long to achieve success or why you haven't settled, or you might have just thought that you're not good enough. Always monitor your thoughts and take notice of the negative thoughts. When you catch a negative view early enough, it is easy to amend it. For example, instead of thinking, I'm not good enough to use a mantra, you want to think, and I'm a great person!

Choose positive explanations

No matter how your actions appear conventionally terrible, you can always rationalize them. For instance, if you had a child while you're still young, instead of looking at it as throwing your dreams away, look at it as bringing something new into the world. The same case applies to your thoughts. On the occasions that you experience negative thoughts, you want to find a positive or realistic explanation.

### List Down the things that you're Grateful for

It is quite easy to overlook the many positive things about your life when you are battling negative thoughts. To shift your mindset from negativity into positivity, you have to list down what you are grateful for. Some of the things that you ought to be grateful to include family, lovers, pets, and home. Whenever you fall short of your expectations, think about what you already have, and close the door to negative thinking patterns.

### Practice mindfulness

Instead of getting lost in the negative thoughts roaming in your mind, learn to shift your focus to the present. Pay direct attention to the things that you are doing at that moment, such as eating, drinking, and other daily activities.

### Seek Guidance and Support

Don't bury yourself in negative thinking patterns. If you have tried in vain to get rid of your unhelpful thoughts, don't feel shy to reach out to an authority for help. They understand your problem probably more than you ever will. Get close to people too. You'd be amazed at the number of kind-hearted people out there ready to help you if you choose to want their help.

# Chapter 5.  Break Your Negative Thought Patterns

During your day, you have more automatic thoughts than you can imagine. These can range from noticing someone's shirt color to registering when a person decides to merge into your lane while driving. And you instinctively slow just enough to give the driver enough space to pass you. These automatic thoughts are snap judgments that influence your behavior without taking up your conscious thought processes. By not focusing on these automatic behaviors, you are free to worry about more complicated thoughts that require more cognition instead, such as worrying about your work deadline or how you will schedule your evening.

These thoughts come unbidden but are quickly ignored or forgotten, as they are hardly relevant to continue about your day. You do not think about why you need to slow down when approaching a stoplight, nor do you think about how you slow down; you simply do it and continue driving. These involuntary, reactionary thoughts are your automatic thoughts. They can be neutral or somewhere on the positive or negative scale. While these thoughts are meant to be useful, they can sometimes be skewed and become detrimental instead.

When automatic thoughts become detrimental, they are considered negative automatic thoughts. This is one of the types of ideas that CBT seeks to correct. Negative automatic thoughts are mostly unconscious, and they color your perception of what is happening around you. These are underlying thoughts of unworthiness, uselessness, and feeling like unloved, or believing you are unimportant or unintelligent. These thoughts may have been internalized through past experiences, and they color your perception of everything. Any time something goes wrong, your automatic negative thinking will feel justified. For example, if you take a wrong turn on your way to a new restaurant to meet someone, you might immediately tell yourself, "Wow, of course, I messed that up and missed my turn! I can't even follow my GPS right without messing something up. Now I'm late, and my friend is going to be angry." Things could have been just fine leading up to that moment, but as soon as you made a mistake, you beat yourself up.

That diatribe is an example of the behavior caused by an automatic negative thought. In that instance, the intuitive negative thought was likely feelings of worthlessness or feeling unintelligent. The automatic negative thinking is your automatic reaction of beating yourself up at any signs of perceived failure. The undertone to the thought is that you believe you are worthless, unintelligent, and unwanted. If you had told yourself, "I am stupid, and no one likes me," you would likely recognize that that is an incorrect statement, but that is the implication when you said what you did to yourself. These negative automatic thoughts can result in reacting in over-the-top fashions, such as screaming at a waiter who drops a cup, or breaking into tears because you accidentally forgot to message something silly and unimportant to a friend when you originally told her you would. CBT will teach you how to identify and correct these thoughts with a variety of different skills.

### Cognitive Distortions

Like negative automatic thoughts, cognitive distortions are automatic thoughts. Still, they are distorted or patently false in some way, shape, or form. These are beliefs you may hold and take at face value, but something about them is inaccurate. Think of this like logic: If a logical argument is unsound, it is essentially worthless and can be discarded based on being unsound. For example, the argument, "If I hop three times right now, then the volcano will suddenly erupt. I hopped three times; therefore, the volcano is blowing up," is logically valid, meaning that the structure of the argument follows the logical rule pattern known as modus ponens. However, anyone can look at that argument and recognize that it is nonsense, even if it follows the pattern. Just as arguments can be unsound or unreasonable, so too can beliefs about the world.

These cognitive distortions can be anything from seeing your neighbor in a foul mood, and automatically deciding it is your fault. You somehow manage to rationalize the jump from point a to b, using cognitive distortions. Because your beliefs at their core are what is flawed, you have no issues accepting it quicker than you would accept the nonsense argument about hopping and volcanoes erupting. It fits the very logical pattern you have developed and fits into your argument, so you see no reason to give it a second thought or challenge it, even if it leaves you feeling down about yourself, anxious, or angry.

These cognitive distortions can be identified, though it does require time and effort. They typically follow specific patterns or fallacies. Because of that, if you analyze your deepest core beliefs, you will begin to identify which of them have become distorted.

## Cognitive Restructuring

Cognitive restructuring is the process of altering your way of thinking. CBT recognizes that thoughts, feelings, and actions are an endless cycle in which thoughts influence feelings, which influence actions, which in turn influence thoughts.

Everything you do feeds into this endless cycle. CBT seeks to disrupt this cycle to change it. For example, imagine you are someone with an anger problem. You often think about things negatively, which keeps you in a negative mood, which causes you to lash out in anger, which only makes you think even more negatively about whatever triggered the outburst in the first place.

CBT interrupts one of those aspects, typically either thoughts or actions, which upsets the entire cycle. For example, if the cause of the angry outburst was that you disliked a restaurant that your family chose to go to for dinner, so you were already in a bad mood when you walked in the door, which contributed to your explosion, CBT would likely seek to change your negative thought. Instead of being annoyed at the restaurant, CBT would have you instead focus on the positive aspect of the event, such as going to dinner with your family and enjoying the occasion, even if the food is not your favorite. By focusing on enjoying your family, you are likely to be in a better mood, which makes you less inclined to react explosively in anger. This cognitive restructuring is used a lot in challenging both negative automatic thoughts and cognitive distortions.

### Core Beliefs

Core beliefs are the beliefs you hold about yourself. They can be either negative or positive, but they color every interaction you have with others and how you perceive the world around you. These core beliefs are largely unconscious, but they can be identified through plenty of introspection and self-reflection. These beliefs are typically developed over a long period, typically beginning in childhood, or through significant life events. These are typically rigid beliefs. You will react according to them, even going so far as to unconsciously force what is happening around you to fit into the core beliefs while denying or disregarding anything that would contradict it.

For example, someone with depression may look at every negative interaction he has as a sign that he is unworthy of love or worthless to everyone around him. However, he will be virtually blind to every instance of those who care about him going out of their way to show they care, such as sending him a silly text of a meme they say on the internet that they know he will appreciate or having his favorite food delivered to him on his birthday.

These core beliefs can be cognitive distortions or colored by negative automatic thoughts, which are important to understand. Once you understand how you feel about yourself, you can decide whether you like how you feel. If you do, you know you are secure with yourself. If you do not, you can begin the steps of cognitive restructuring to alter them.

### Emotional Triggers

Sometimes, something around us suddenly triggers an overwhelming sense of negative emotion. You could have been happily chatting with someone, and at the drop of a hat, suddenly felt your blood boiling, your pulse racing, and like you cannot decide between screaming at someone or punching them. This reaction is called being emotionally triggered. You may know during, or after the fact that your reaction is irrational and disproportionate. Still, despite that, you cannot control it. The best you can do is seek to understand what your emotional trigger is so you can plan a way to avoid blowing up in the future.

Emotional triggers are typically related to some sort of trauma that has caused you to internalize a strong reaction to things reminiscent of the trauma. Someone who suffered through an abusive relationship might be triggered by someone saying a common phrase if it was one the abusive partner said regularly. The sound of barking may trigger someone traumatized by a dog attack at a young age. Someone home from war may be triggered by loud sounds reminiscent of explosions or gunfire.

Understanding what your emotional triggers are will help you begin the cognitive restructuring process to retrain yourself from being less reactive to them. If you are aware that you react negatively to people with beards that surprise you, there are methods you can use to desensitize yourself, so your reactions are not as strong or negative. Through a combination of cognitive restructuring and exposure to your trigger in a controlled environment, you will be able to overcome these emotional triggers and stop allowing them to rule your life.

# Chapter 6.   How to Identify Your Core Beliefs

We looked at ways to discover and change our negative automatic thoughts. We are going to explore what drives those negative thoughts. Why do our minds produce those thinking patterns so quickly and effortlessly? We'll delve deeper into the nature of our thought processes and find there are deep-seated beliefs that underlie our everyday thoughts and modify through CBT.

The concept of a core belief captures the idea that our negative automatic thoughts are not random. When we pay attention to what our minds are doing, we'll find themes that recur again and again. The specific topics will vary for each of us; our typical responses to triggering situations will reveal our own core beliefs.

A core belief is like a radio station—the songs may differ, but they belong to the same genre: country, jazz, hip-hop, or classical, for example. When you're tuned to a station, you know what kind of songs to expect. In the same way, our core beliefs cue up predictable thoughts. For example, Simon's core belief of being unappreciated triggered negative automatic thoughts about others' lack of gratitude.

By noticing the "tracks" that your mind often plays, you'll discover what frequency you're tuned to. With practice, you can develop the ability to change the station.

## Why Do We Have Core Beliefs?

Our brains have to process an incredible amount of information. Imagine you're walking in a big city looking for a restaurant where you're meeting a friend. When you enter the restaurant, your senses will be bombarded with countless stimuli—people standing, others sitting, various rooms, and so forth. If you had to process each stimulus consciously, it would take an enormous amount of time to figure out the setup.

Fortunately, our minds contain "maps" that help us quickly make sense of the situation, assuming it's not the first time we've been in a restaurant. We know the host, who greets us, so we explain that we're meeting a friend who will be joining us shortly. We're not the least bit surprised when the host hands us a piece of paper after we sit down, which we know will list the food items and drinks and the price for each. Our entire meal will unfold predictably by paying the check and saying good-bye to the host on the way out.

This example shows that our brains develop shortcuts based on prior learning. Once we know an individual experience, we can navigate it efficiently. This ability indicates that we bring organized knowledge to the experience, relying on an internal model that guides our behavior.

In just the same way, our minds developmental structures that help us deal with potentially emotional situations like rejection, success, failure, and so forth. For example, if we experience a small fault, like missing our train and being late to a meeting, we might think we're irresponsible and respond with feelings of guilt and regret. We might enter the meeting tentatively and with words and a demeanor that suggest not just "I'm sorry" but also, "I've done something bad." These thoughts, feelings, and behaviors emanate from the core belief I am inadequate. Being late for the meeting didn't cause that belief so much as confirm it: "See, here's yet another example of how I'm defective."

Maintaining a different core belief would give rise to a very unusual cluster of responses. If I believe on a fundamental level that I'm a person of worth, I may see my tardiness as regrettable but not indicative of my overall value. I would undoubtedly experience less stress on my commute to work since my worth as a human being doesn't hinge on whether I'm on time. Even if my boss pointed out that I'm late, it wouldn't have a significant impact on how I felt about myself.

### Identifying Your Core Beliefs

Think about the negative automatic thoughts that often come up for you. Do you notice any repetitive messages?

You can record those thoughts in the outer ring of the figure displayed here if you've worked on identifying and changing your automatic thoughts.

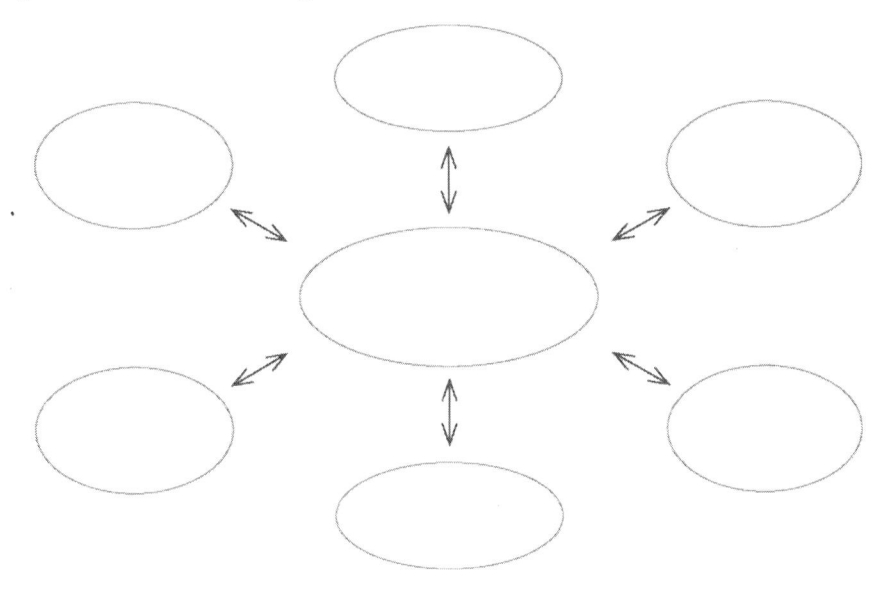

As you consider these automatic thoughts, do you find a central belief that unites them all? If so, write it in the space in the middle. For example, Esther had a lot of anxiety about her health. She completed the core belief diagram below:

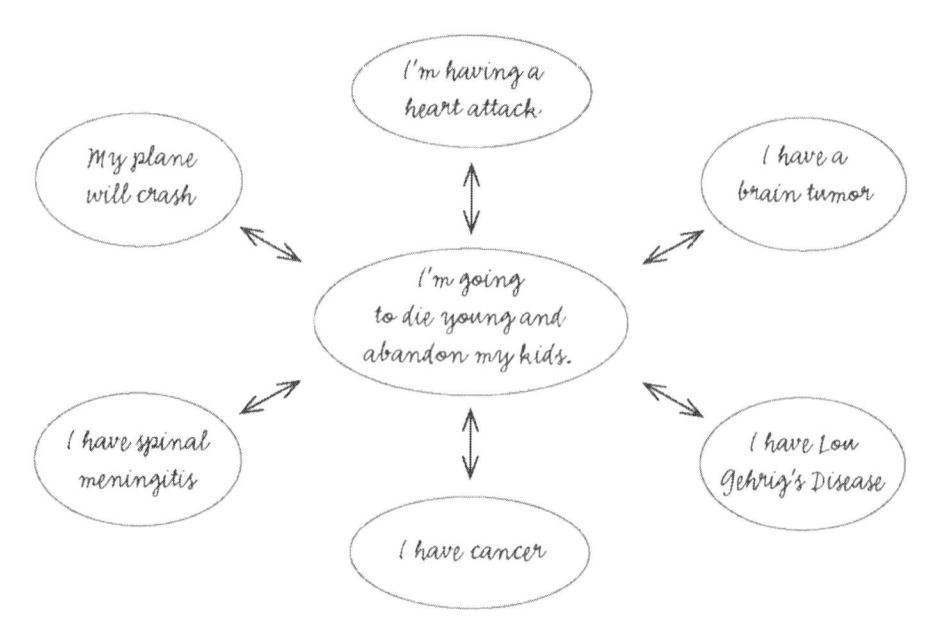

```
         I'm having a
          heart attack
              ↕
My plane                    I have a
will crash                  brain tumor
        ↘              ↙
           I'm going
        to die young and
        abandon my kids.
        ↗              ↖
I have spinal     ↕         I have Lou
meningitis                  Gehrig's Disease
           I have cancer
```

When Esther flew on a plane, she interpreted every bump of turbulence as a sign of an imminent crash. We might expect that many safe landings would weaken her fear of flying since they provide evidence against her fear. However, core beliefs act as a filter that only lets in the information that confirms our suspicions. Each time Esther flew, she had automatic thoughts like "We're losing altitude!" that made her think she had narrowly escaped an untimely death. Rather than feeling safer, she was convinced that she might not be so lucky the other time.

As Esther learned, core beliefs and automatic thoughts act in a self-perpetuating manner, each being the cause and the consequence of the other. As you become more aware of your patterns of thinking, be on the lookout for instances when your core beliefs are interfering with an objective take on reality. This process requires paying close attention to the presence of thinking errors in specific situations, taking care not to believe everything our minds tell us.

Keep in mind that negative core beliefs can lie dormant when we're feeling well and emerge when we're gripped by strong emotion. Individuals prone to depression are especially likely to show an increase in negative beliefs when they experience a negative mood, raising the risk for future episodes of depression. Thankfully we can train our minds to guard against relapse, as individuals who have used CBT show a smaller increase in negative thinking during low moods.

You can also use the downward arrow technique to get to your core beliefs. At each step, ask yourself what it would mean if your thought were right.

Esther used the downward arrow technique to examine the implications of her automatic thought about having cancer:

You can use the top-down arrow technique to explore your own core beliefs.

## Where Do Our Core Beliefs Come From?

A significant part of the tendency to experience negative emotions—what personality researchers call "neuroticism"—depends on our genes, and research has shown that core beliefs are tied to our levels of neuroticism. It's unlikely that genetic differences account for the specific core beliefs we hold. These particular beliefs depend on our life experiences.

Sophie constantly battles feelings of being not good enough in some way. She's had this feeling for as long as she can remember and recalls a similar feeling from as early as kindergarten. She had struggled with ADHD as a child, and although she was very bright, she had been late learning to read. Her parents had her repeat kindergarten when she moved to school districts to give her a chance to catch up with her peers.

Sophie's little sister Claire, in contrast, was reading before age five, and her parents frequently praised Claire for her calm behavior and success in school. As an adult now looking back, Sophie suspects her feelings of inadequacy are based in part on the disappointment she sensed from her parents and her belief that they loved Claire more than they loved her.

A single event of parental disapproval or mild teasing is unlikely to leave a lasting mark. However, a general pattern of treatment will probably shape the way individuals view the world and themselves. If the event is sufficiently traumatic, even a single episode can shape our beliefs. For example, one assault can shift our views on how safe the world is, just as an only betrayal can alter our ability to trust others.

We can also develop core beliefs based on things we observed as we were growing up. For example, if we witnessed our father is always stressed out about finances, we may have developed a core belief about economic scarcity. Or if our mother was continually warning us to be careful, we could develop a core belief about the world as a place of constant threat.

Some of the beliefs we developed earlier in life may have made sense at the time but are less useful now. For example, a boy who grew up with an abusive parent might have learned that standing up for himself only led to more abuse. As a result, he developed the core belief I am helpless, which reflected the powerlessness of his situation. Decades after this belief may persist, even though he is no longer a dependent child.

Take some time to think about your history. Are there any events that stand out as possible contributors to your core beliefs? What were the predominant family dynamics as you were growing up? What were you taught earlier in life, intentionally or not? And how might these experiences have affected your views of the world, other people, and yourself? Take some time to write your thoughts in your journal.

# Chapter 7. Change Your Core Beliefs

You want to move ahead in life and find fulfillment. You cannot see this if you have beliefs that hold you back. To successfully eliminate these limiting beliefs, the following strategies should be of help:

Loudly, read out your opinion and ask yourself if you know that it is true.

Check if you have experienced it many times to make it right. Keep in mind, concluding limited experiences will not give you the correct answer. Ensure that you have no doubts whatsoever in establishing the belief to be true.

It is not possible for a person without money to tell how to have it and the consequences of having it. You must also establish if the origin of your belief is credible or not. Ideas are developed from personal experiences and expert advice. Rely on information from experts to change your mindset.

Make a simple, bold statement and decide not to believe the belief you hold anymore because it is not valid.

When a person boldly states their intention, and it usually has a great impact on their lives. To reinforce that your belief is false, look for evidence that supports this fact, such as:

- Whoever told you that has no experience or knowledge on the subject
- You have relied on other people's experience yet you have never tried it to know
- Against all the odds, others that were more disadvantaged than you have succeeded and you have witnessed it

If you think on those lines, you will begin to doubt the validity of the limiting belief you have held. Research and read more on the subject that you feel your ideas are limiting and see how you can change. Visualize changing your life by eliminating the belief.

### Come up with a new Belief that is Beneficial.

For every limiting belief, come up with an opposite view. Come up with the idea that will improve your life and motivate you to improve your experience. Do this by getting evidence that supports your new positive belief. This helps to create stability for your understanding.

For every new belief, make sure you get evidence to support it to be true.

### Evaluate Yourself

With each day, consider performing a proper audit on yourself. Evaluate how you feel with the new belief. How do you think about your opinion? What is your gut instinct regarding the original idea? Do you feel that your behavior is changing?

Be genuine with the response you come up with. If you can change your beliefs, how you behave and feel will change. Each person's life is a manifestation of his or her feelings. When you genuinely change your expectations, you will also be able to transform your life fully.

Keep going back to your list of beliefs and keep changing those that influence negatively in your life. As you progress in making the changes, you will discover other limiting beliefs and work on improving them. With each step of your life, you will set new goals that will challenge you differently.

With each new goal you set, evaluate how to get there, the possible obstacles, and what beliefs you have that may limit you from achieving the goals. Make it a habit to continuously evaluate yourself, identify the limiting beliefs, and eliminate them.

### Psychology and Spirituality to Change Your Core Beliefs

Psychology defined as the study of how our mind works and affects our behavior. Psychology as science investigates the causes of actions and can be used to change practices as well.

Spirituality is different from religion. It is about understanding who you are by looking beyond what we see. Spirituality is very central in forming a person's core beliefs.

People's core beliefs affect their outward behavior. Through psychology and spirituality, one can transform their lives into what they visualize. This can be done through a transformation of the mindset.

Most of the issues people encounter are a result of having underlying believes or questions. Both spirituality and psychology look at transforming your thoughts to improve your life.

To change your life, you must begin by completely transforming your mindset. The nature of your thoughts determines the quality of your life. Positive thoughts, optimism, feelings, and emotions generate some form of energy in your system that allows you to have internal joy.

How we act, it is a direct manifestation of our thoughts. Psychology and spirituality work together to bring a change in the way a person thinks and generates happiness and fulfillment in our daily lives.

It is possible to change your thoughts and transform your life. Here is a list of ways that you can use to improve your ideas and transform your life positively.

1. Create positive affirmations

Affirmations can also be harmful. Unfortunately, most people are used to making negative affirmations. When a person repeatedly thinks they are going to fail, it is an example of a negative statement. Both negative and positive affirmations affect the functioning of your brain.

Mantras are examples of positive affirmations. Mantras are almost sacred with a spiritual. When creating positive affirmations, they should not be weak or average.

Examples of negative affirmations are: 'I can't be able. It is impossible.' On the other side, positive affirmations are determined and forceful like 'I can or I will.' Your brain responds to how you think and, as such, directs the rest of the body organs to act as per your thoughts.

2. Know when to stop

Many people like to dwell on the misfortunes they have encountered along the way. The wrongs they perceive were committed against them by their loved ones. They keep cursing themselves because of the mistakes they made and analyzing what they could have done differently.

It is OK to learn from our past and plan to do better in the future. However, it is not healthy to dwell in the past because we forget to move forward with life.

3. Stop being masochistic

Many times people want to wallow in self-pity and misery. We create self-punishing thoughts and enjoy that state of mind; we focus on pessimistic thoughts and being consistently gloomy. Some people will believe they are naturally unlucky, and so nothing good will ever happen in their lives.

These kinds of thoughts are harmful to your mind and equally detrimental to your physical health.

4. <u>Count your blessings and your joys</u>

Don't take your blessings and joy for granted. Stop grumbling every time you are faced with a challenge. You can counter this by always remembering those that are less fortunate in life than you. It is also possible for a situation to have been worse, think about that too.

Practice gratitude to enjoy the fullness of life. When you are grateful, the negatives turn to positives. Where there is chaos, the order becomes. Where there is confusion, clarity becomes. This is only possible by having a grateful attitude.

5. <u>Appreciate what you have</u>

The easiest and most excellent way to transform your thoughts is by enjoying and appreciating what you have. Instead of feeling sad because of what you have not achieved in life yet, try being appreciative of where you are now.

Fixing your eyes on more important things is good. However, to reach those great heights, you must begin where you are and enjoy it. If you don't achieve your goals, appreciate what you have so far, and it will motivate you to make more.

6. <u>Enjoy your achievements</u>

Achieving your goals and enjoying them are two different things. Many people set out with goals in mind. As soon as they make them, they become restless and looking for more instead of enjoying what they have achieved. If you aimed to achieve something, follow your goals, and once you do, appreciate the effort and achievement.

7. <u>When trials come, stand tall.</u>

It is natural to feel unmotivated and demoralized when we face challenging conditions. We stop moving and focus on exploring the weight of the challenges. However, try and lift your spirits, and you will feel better.

Hold your head high and, with determination, face the challenges to get out of them successfully.

8. <u>Enjoy the child in you.</u>

Children are pure in their thinking and innocent. They will fight or quarrel with their friends and forget it so fast and start playing together once again. Unfortunately for grownups, we hold issues within us that poison our spirit and minds. As children, it is essential to practice forgiving and to forget an incident as soon as it has happened and talked over.

9. <u>Seek to be happy and contented</u>

Most people associate their happiness with events in the future. They peg their happiness to future happenings, and if those things don't happen, they are no longer happy. Don't postpone your joy; instead, enjoy your moment today because tomorrow does not belong to you.

10. <u>Control your moods</u>

Don't be a servant to your moods; instead, be the master. Remember, you define your happiness. Never allow circumstances or people to dampen your spirit and make you unhappy.

Other people associate their happiness to material possessions; do not attach your pleasure to things. Choose to be happy, regardless of the situation. Don't allow heartbreaks to dominate; you instead find joy under all circumstances.

### 11. Resolve to have a happy day

Every day comes with its challenges and situations that can trigger unhappiness. Wake up every day with a determination to be happy. Identify things that bring you joy and focus on those. Look to nature for inspiration and joy. Purpose to stay calm despite the situations you may face and remain happy.

### 12. Honor your body because it is your temple

Consider your Body to be sacred. Keep it well cleaned and avoid dumping garbage, toxic food, and negative thoughts in it. To stay happy, you must stay healthy, both mentally and physically. Engage in active physical exercises often and read inspiring content that acts to motivate you.

### 13. Learn to meditate daily

Meditation does not have to be complicated, as some people have made it be. Every evening, find a quiet place, focus on how your day was, and pay attention to the good things that made you feel good. If something not so pleasant happened, focus on the lessons you learned from the situation but do not attract negative thoughts by regretting it. By doing this, you fill your mind with gratitude and create a happier you.

### 14. Forget about changing the world but focus on improving yourself

When people fall short of your expectations, do not get upset. You cannot change the world, but the best way is to change how you view the world by changing yourself. By changing yourself, you allow yourself to adjust to the situations around you, and in so doing, you avoid stress.

15. <u>Use what you have and make the best of it</u>

Do not focus your energies on thinking of what the best could be. Instead, take what you have and make the best out of it. The world is not ideal. Forget the imperfections around you. Change your thoughts and change your world.

Thoughts are compelling. Your ideas can be an obstacle to your happiness or the cause of your mental health issues. You are transforming your thoughts results in the transformation of your mindset. When your mind is changed, you live a healthier, happier, and more fulfilling life.

Cognitive-behavioral therapy focuses on transforming your mindset from a negative one to a positive one. Identifying your core beliefs and how they affect your thought pattern is the beginning of your transformation.

# Chapter 8. Eliminate Procrastination and Work through Worry, Fear, and Anxiety

## How CBT Handles Anxiety

Anxiety is the uneasiness an individual may feel about a particular person, object, place, or situation. Sometimes taking shape as fear or worry, the concern is such a familiar feeling that comes and goes in everyone's lifetime.

However, some develop certain kinds of anxiety disorders that can lead to having extreme and irrational reactions or behavioral responses. Anxiety disorders are psychiatric problems that can make an individual feel intense negative emotion that may lead to unfavorable circumstances.

There are six major kinds of anxiety disorders, all of which involve certain types of anxiety and different ways of how it is triggered and addressed. Many mental health professionals widely regard Cognitive-Behavioral Therapy (CBT) as the preferred psychosocial intervention for most of them.

Aside from its impressive effectiveness, it also helps the individual lead a better life even with the disorder. It teaches them a lot of valuable skills that will help them cope with their conditions. Listed below are some of the anxiety disorders and how CBT can help individuals overcome each one.

## Generalized Anxiety Disorder (GAD)

One of the most prevalent anxiety disorders around, Generalized Anxiety Disorder (GAD) is characterized by excessive worry about almost everything in a person's life with no particular cause or reason as to why.

Individuals who have GAD tend to make a big deal out of everything. They become anxious about everything in their life — be it their financial status, work, family, friends, or health — and are always preoccupied with worries that something terrible might happen. They expect the worst-case scenario about everything and always try to look at things from a negative point of view.

With that said, it's easy to see how GAD can make it difficult for someone to live a happy and healthy life. It can come as a hindrance to their day-to-day life and become an issue with regards to their work, family, friends, and any other social activities. Some of the most common symptoms of GAD include excessive worry or tension, tiredness, inability to rest, difficulty sleeping, headaches, mood swings, difficulty in concentrating, and nausea.

Fortunately, however, CBT has worked wonders in treating all these symptoms and more. With the help of CBT, individuals suffering from GAD can change negative thoughts to positive ones, which will improve their behaviors for the better.

There are several CBT techniques that people with GAD can apply to manage their symptoms better. For example, if you have GAD and want to feel relief from all the muscle

tension in your body, you can try yoga; whereas meditation can help you stop overthinking; and breathing exercises are functional to practice when you start to feel yourself getting anxious again.

Yoga has been proven to help lower a person's stress, which in turn, relaxes their muscles. There are several different yoga poses and routines you can find on the internet tailored to relieving your stress and anxiety. Some examples include the eagle pose, the headstand, child's pose, half-moon pose, and the legs up the wall pose.

If you need help getting started with how to use yoga to ease some of the distress you may feel from GAD, here is a quick rundown of how you can do it:

- Go to the gym and sign up for their yoga class.
- Or if you prefer, you can stay at home and do yoga by yourself.
- It's often best to do yoga in the afternoon or at the end of the day, as a way to decompress.
- Set up your mat, and if you want, play some relaxing music.
- Breathe in and out, deeply.
- Be aware of your breathing as you move through each pose.
- Take your time going through all the movements.
- Most importantly, enjoy yourself and keep your mind clear.

On the other hand, if the most problematic symptom of your GAD is overthinking and emotional turmoil, not muscle tension and chronic pain, then meditation just might be the CBT technique for you. Here's how you can do it:

- Download some guided meditation videos online (there's plenty on YouTube).
- Listen to them regularly, preferably every day (as you wake up or go to sleep is the most ideal).
- Find a quiet place to do this, where you can be alone and away from distractions.
- Devote all your attention to these 10-30 minute meditations. Do not think or worry about anything else while you're doing so.

- Make it a rule that once you start meditating, you need to forget about everything going on in your life and just focus on the present moment.
- Repeat everything the instructor is saying in the guided meditation.

By meditating, you are giving your anxiety a healthy and positive outlet and releasing your physical tension from your body. The more you do it, the more peace you will feel, and the easier it will be for you to overcome your anxiety.

When using CBT, a person with GAD will have a much more favorable perspective in life. Instead of always worrying and thinking about the worst-case scenario, CBT reinforces an optimistic and reasonable outlook on life, which will have a positive impact on their behavior as well. Most of the time, they'll change from a tense and edgy person to a relaxed and easygoing one that doesn't assume the worst out of everything.

### Social Anxiety

Another common type of anxiety is social anxiety, characterized by immediate distress whenever you meet or interact with unfamiliar people. Affecting over 15 million different American adults can be considered one of the most prominent types of anxiety in the country.

Also known as "social phobia," those with social anxiety often display visible signs or symptoms that indicate their discomfort towards the situation. Some of those symptoms may include blushing, stuttering, increased heart rate, sweating, awkwardness or annoyance, and, worst-case scenario, experiencing a full-blown anxiety attack.

If you are one of the many people suffering from social anxiety than you'd understand how much of a disturbance it can be in your life. Because it hinders you from a lot of social interactions, you may have a hard time connecting with other people and making new friends. This may also affect your personality, as it can keep you from enjoying yourself when you're out with friends since you don't dare to stand up and talk for yourself. You fear to become involved in social situations and try your best to keep to yourself as much as possible and avoid interacting with other people.

Although individuals with social anxiety know that their reaction to the situation may be over-the-top or unreasonable, they just can't seem to keep the stress and emotions at bay. They often seem powerless when battling this emotion, and sometimes, in the end, anxiety takes over their lives. Due to these symptoms, they may try their best to avoid situations where they might get pressured into socializing with other people at all costs.

To overcome social anxiety, many individuals have turned to therapy. Cognitive Behavioral Therapy (CBT) is one of the most common and used treatments for this particular problem. With an array of different methods and techniques, CBT can help you overcome your social anxiety by getting to the heart of the problem: your thoughts.

Everything we feel and do stems from our thoughts. So, CBT alters the way individuals process information and turns negative thoughts into positive ones. In turn, it generates positive moods that may also lead to favorable actions or behavior. When relating CBT to social anxiety, it tries to get rid of all the negative thoughts that may pop into your mind when you're about to interact with other people.

For example, when you're meeting new people, you might instantly think that they might hate you or dislike the way you talk or act immediately. However, with CBT, it eliminates this type of thinking. It keeps an open and positive mindset of the things that may happen. CBT can also help individuals calm themselves when experiencing a panic attack or when having an inner conflict colored with anxiety.

Some CBT techniques are specially designed to help individuals overcome different types of situations. For example, Cognitive Restructuring can be used in treating social phobia. It can be crucial to understand your triggers, control your mood swings, and keep a positive mindset on everything.

Typically, individuals would have to go to therapists for their own CBT treatment. However, there are some ways that it can still help you when you're on your own. You simply have to follow a series of steps to overcome the situation.

- Make an effort to calm yourself down before you interact with someone else.
- Look at the current situation you're faced with. Describe it to yourself.
- Assess how that particular situation made you feel and identify those feelings.
- Go through your thoughts on that specific scenario and scan through what your mind immediately thought of when you faced that situation. The first few thoughts that pop into your head are your "automatic thoughts."
- Narrow in on your negative automatic thoughts. Ask yourself what triggered these thoughts.

Now, are these triggers reasonable? Is it your negative view of yourself or the situation justifiable? Be as objective as you can and try not to let your emotions get in the way.

Soon, you will realize that your thoughts are only misguided and aren't true at all. They're just the lies you sometimes tell yourself which feed your insecurity.

Work on erasing these thoughts from your mind by replacing them with the truth. For example, whenever you think, "Nobody likes me," automatically reply with, "Hey! That's just not true! [This certain person] likes me!"

Cognitive restructuring can be beneficial for individuals trying to control or assess how they react to specific scenarios. It can help them lighten their mood.

AS for those individuals who still need to calm their nerves whenever they are faced with a situation they dread so much, they can also try relaxation techniques. While we've already talked a lot about yoga, meditation, and breathing exercises to help you relax, here is another method you can use to calm yourself down:

- Take a seat and sit with your back straight.
- Place one hand along your chest and the other one on your stomach.
- Inhale through your nose. You will notice your hand on your stomach area moves more while your other hand should only move slightly.
- Breathe out with your mouth. This will cause your stomach to move in while your chest will still move slightly.
- Repeat this process and count each deep breath you take. Imagine that with every exhale, you are releasing negative energy from your body.
- After a while, your muscle tension will decrease, and you will feel a lot calmer than beforehand. Keep doing this until you no longer feel any distress or anxiety.

## Panic Disorder

Panic attacks are characterized by out-of-the-blue emotions or feelings of trepidation when, in fact, there is no real reason to be afraid. Having recurrent panic attacks for seemingly no reason at all is what is known as a panic disorder. This is mostly found in young adults aged 20 and above. However, it can also be experienced by other children who also have panic-like symptoms.

Anxiety disorders can significantly affect a person's life. Always being at risk of spontaneous panic attacks may lead them to avoid going out, and thus, isolate themselves from others. Individuals with the panic disorder typically live in fear of getting another panic attack, so they try their best to control it or maybe even hide from other people.

# Chapter 9. Practice Mindfulness

There's no way that you could learn a new skill without any form of guidance or instruction. Imagine you're given the keys to a Ferrari, and you're asked to drive it in heavy traffic, but you've never forced a day in your life. That would not work out well. The same thing applies when it comes to mindfulness. If it were merely telling you, "Go forth and be mindful," then I had better wrap up this here because there's nothing else to do, I guess. Don't worry. I'm not going to leave you hanging.

At the core of Dialectical Behavioral Therapy is mindfulness. We're going to take a look at each of the steps you need to go through to practice mindfulness. It's not enough to know it can help you. I want to empower you with the knowledge you need to save yourself.

Now, you may be a tad skeptical of all of this. Perhaps more than a few times already, you have considered setting this aside, because you find it inconceivable that only learning mindfulness as a skill could be all you need to turn your life around. It's not unusual for BPD patients to be skeptical of the whole thing. For a problem as complex as BPD, how could anyone even suggest something as simple and basic as mindfulness? What the heck does "mindfulness" also mean anyway? Full of mind? You're tempted to assume it's some religious hokey by Buddhists, and so you should not pay it any attention. There is no way all your problems could be resolved by merely breathing, you think. These are all logical thoughts.

It's natural to raise a brow in suspicion at the whole concept, especially when you have no idea what it means to practice mindfulness, or how you would begin in the first place.

## Laying the Groundwork

You're probably trying to figure out how often and for how long you should practice being mindful each time. Since you're only just starting, you should begin with just 15 to 20 minutes a day. You can easily split that up into two sessions, once at the start of your day, and once at the end.

As you get used to your practice, you could begin to add on a bit of time to your sessions each day. We're going to cover ways in which you can be mindful all through your day. Still, we're also going to cover the basics of picking a set time each day for a more focused, formal session. This is important because being deliberate about it is the only way you can be mindful. One more thing I ought to mention is that no matter how good you become aware of yourself, you must make sure you keep up your practice day after day.

This is not a prerequisite. Find a time that is convenient for you and commit to it. If you find that you're exhausted at the end of your day, then you definitely would be better off practicing in the afternoon or the morning. If you have to start your mornings early and have a lot to do to prepare your family for the day, you might want to consider noon or night for practice. It's all up to you. The point is that you must make it a habit, and remember, the only way habits are formed constant repetition. Do what you need to make it happen. Leave yourself a note somewhere you'll always pass by, remember, or set a reminder on your phone.

If it's a seated mindfulness practice, then it would be best to adopt a posture where your chest is open, meaning you keep your arms away from your chest. You also want to make sure that your bottom is firmly and evenly planted on the seat. Choose a good chai, which allows you to sit up comfortably. If you need a few pillows to support your back, then use them.

Make sure your feet are flat on the floor, firmly and evenly. Do not cross your ankles or your legs. Your shoulders must be back and upright. Don't hunch over. You may keep your arms on your lap. If you like, you can turn your palms upwards. A considerable part of this mindfulness practice is also aware of your posture as you sit. Now that you know how to sit, you're going to practice while keeping your eyes open.

## Owning Your Mind

The more you practice mindfulness, the more you'll find that you own your mind. You are more in control of it. Right now, I can see how you'd think this is an impossible feat. However, it's true! As you practice, you will discover you are not your emotions or your thoughts, but something more.

For the most part, people tend to ignore how much of a habit thought patterns are. We never really think about our thinking, because we weren't taught how to do that. This is where mindfulness can help again. If your mind is not trained, it can cause you a lot of pain and heartache without you even being aware of it. Like a pendulum, you swing from one extreme to the other. You either get so enmeshed in your mind that you pay way too much attention to specific thoughts or worry about the point of obsession and are unable to see past your nose. Either way, you don't pay attention to your thinking habits. It almost seems to you that things tend to unfold on their own, and you have no power over how you react. I don't need to tell you how being on one extreme or the other can cause you issues, and suffering. Mindfulness will help you grow in curiosity, awareness, and attention. This is how you'll finally own your mind and break the habits of thought you've got.

## The Need for Curiosity and Attentiveness

When you don't develop your attention, and when you're not curious about life, you'll be stuck in your usual routines. Routines may help you avoid the pain you feel, but in the end, they also keep you stuck, and this can add to more pain in the long run. It never pays to try to ignore your emotions and thoughts.

You have to pay attention to your thoughts. This means you need to pause now and then and take an unbiased look at your mind. How fast or slow are you thinking? Are your thoughts a jumbled mess or well put together? Are they loving and kind or angry and resentful? What exactly is it that you're thinking about?

The point of mindfulness is to take charge of your mind and thought processes, and by extension, your emotions. AS you pay attention, the peace and serenity you feel in your life will go up a hundredfold. It might be difficult to believe that mindfulness can help you achieve all this, especially as you've never done it before, but I promise you it works.

## The Practice

As you practice, pay attention to how your body and mind feel. This will help you learn all the things you can do to decrease your suffering through your emotions and thoughts. In the DBT space, these actions are known as the "what" and "how" skills — "what" being the actions you take to be mindful, and "how" being the way you go about it.

Try the practices that you will be given in this at least one time. You'll need a journal so that you can take down notes on your experiences after each practice. You will find that some of the practices feel better for you than others, however, don't stick to them just yet without trying everything, so that you can tell what works for you and what doesn't. The goal isn't to get you to like the practice, but to encourage you to become more curious, and give your mind a challenge.

One more thing I should mention is that your mind will wander. You must be comfortable with that fact. When you notice your mind has gone off on a tangent, do not beat up on yourself. Noticing is progress! So simply bring your mind back to your mindful task, whatever it may be. Each time your mind wanders, and you bring it back, you will get better at maintaining mindfulness. Remember, your mind is like a muscle. This is how it gets stronger.

### The Power of Intention

You cannot practice mindfulness without intention. The intention is a beautiful thing, because if you can do something mindlessly, then with intention, you can do it mindfully. Intention means you're choosing to pay attention to something, with a specific goal in mind. So you could brush your teeth like always, while your thoughts are on autopilot, wondering about bills and mortgages, or you can spend that time noticing the way you brush, the way your mouth feels, and so on. You notice the desire to think about how to take care of the bills, but then you shift your attention back to the simple act of brushing your teeth. As you brush, your mind will wander off. When it does, you can simply come back to brushing. You can do this with any activity that you do on the regular, whether it's driving, walking, doing the dishes, or laundry. This is how you infuse mindfulness in your daily activities.

There is a misconception that the whole point of mindfulness is to have a mind that never wanders. That's impossible. You will always have thoughts in your head. That's the function of your brain. What mindfulness is, is intentionally choosing to refocus your attention back on the tasks at hand each time your mind wanders. It's not about keeping your mind quiet and empty.

### Decide, Commit, Succeed

As you decide to practice being mindful, you've got to keep reminding yourself of what you've set out to do and why. It matters that in the beginning, you are clear about the fact that you're going to be mindful of the task you've chosen, whether it's doing the dishes or washing your car. Tell yourself you will do this mindfully, and automatically your brain takes a cue that it needs to focus on the task before you. Once you commit this way, you are more likely to succeed.

### A Different Practice for Each Day

All you need to do is intend to change at least one of the things you do habitually for every day, just for a week. Try getting out on the right if you're used to getting out of bed on the left side. Do you usually open doors with your dominant hand? Commit to using the other hand. It's all about doing something different for a set period and paying full attention to the process.

# Chapter 10.   Managing Excessive Anger

### Steps to Take in Managing Anger

In life, many things may be out of one's control. These things vary from the weather, the past, other people, intrusive thoughts, physical sensations, and one's own emotions. Despite all these, the power to choose is always disposable to any human. Even though one might not be able to control the weather, one can decide whether to wear heavy clothing. One can also choose how to respond to other people.

### A "Should" Rule is Broken

Everybody has some rules and expectations for one's behavior, and also for other people's behavior. Some of these rules include, "I should be able to do this," "She should not treat me like this," and, "They should stay out of my way." Unfortunately, no one has control over someone else's actions. Therefore, these rules are always bound to be broken, and people may get in one's way. This can result in anger, guilt, and pressure.

It is, therefore, essential first break these "should" rules to fight this anger. The first step to make in breaking these rules is to accept the reality of life that someone usually has very little control over other people's lives. The additional step is for one to choose a direction based on one's values. How does one know their benefits? One can identify their values by what angers them, frustrates them, or even enrages them. For example, let's take the rule of "They should stay out of my way." This rule may mean the values of communication, progress, or even cooperation.

- What do these values mean to someone?
- Does one have control over them?

- What does one want in the long run?

Finally, one can act by their values. To help with this, here are two questions one should ask themselves:

- What constructive steps can one take in that direction?
- What Hurts?

The second step is to find the real cause of pain or fear after breaking the rules. These rules usually do not mean the same because some states of being can hurt one's self-esteem more than others.

Let's take the example of Maryah, who expects no one to talk ill of her to understand this better. Then suddenly, Kelvin comes up to her and says all manner of things to her. This, therefore, makes Maryah enraged. In such a scenario, Maryah should ask herself what hurts her. The answer to this question will bring out a general belief about Kelvin and herself. She will think that "Kelvin is rude," "She is powerless," or even that "She is being made the victim." All these thoughts may hurt her. What may also destroy her most is that she has no control over Kelvin's behavior.

Once she has noted that she has no control, she may now consider seeing Kelvin's words as a mere opinion rather than an insult. This will make her not see herself as a victim, but as a person just receiving a piece of someone else's mind about herself.

### Hot Thoughts

After, one has identified what hurts them, it is now time to identify and, most importantly, replace the hot, anger-driven, and reactive thoughts with more level-headed, more relaxed, and reflective thoughts. Here are some fresh ideas that may be of importance to someone:

> Hot thought: "How mean can he be!"
- ✓ Cool thought: "He thinks he is so caring."
> Hot thought: "They are stupid!"
- ✓ Cool thought: "They are just human."

All The above steps, as one may have noticed, relate to the thoughts. This is because one has first to tackle the ideas before now getting to the emotion. In this step, therefore, one is going to respond to the anger arousal itself. There are three ways that one can follow to respond to this emotion:

One may indulge in relaxation. This relaxation can come in many forms, like enjoying some music, practicing some progressive muscle relaxation like yoga, and also visualization.

One may also use that feeling to do some constructive work. When one is angry, there is usually a large amount of energy that one uses at that time. This is why, when angry, they can break down things that they would never break when calm. Imagine, therefore, how much that energy would do for someone if just directed to some constructive work.

One may also try to redefine anger when one gets angry. What does this mean? Once a person is angry, one can try to remind themselves of how violence is a problem that fuels aggression and can cause harm to loved ones and even oneself.

## Moral Disengagement

This step will help one examine the beliefs that turn anger into aggression. These beliefs usually act as mere excuses or justification for destructive acts. Some of these beliefs include "I don't care," "This is the only way I can get my point across," or even "It is high time they recognize me." These beliefs need to be identified early enough and gotten rid of before they can con one into throwing one's morals aside. One sure way of getting rid of them is by reminding oneself of the cost of such beliefs and the advantages of striving for understanding.

### Aggression

In This step, one now needs to examine the behaviors that arise from aggression and try to fight them. Fighting these behaviors can be achieved if one calms down and puts oneself in another person's shoes. This will help one understand why the other person is acting in such a manner, what they may be feeling, or even what they may be thinking. This approach will help to:

Decrease the anger for all parties involved.

Increase the chance of having a reasonable conversation with the parties involved, and thus everybody is heard.

### Outcome

The final step of this procedure is to reduce resentment towards others, and also guilt towards oneself.

## Step 1: Choose a triggering situation

By now, you already know the things that trigger anger, anxiety, and upsetting feelings for you. Try to put them down on paper and select one that is least challenging to you just for starters. The reason why we begin with the least challenging is so that you can practice your skills successfully one at a time until you can face your worst fears.

This may take days to weeks, hence the need for patience. Try to stretch yourself out of your comfort zone while ensuring that you do not get overwhelmed. However, if you feel that this process is emotionally overwhelming, you must seek help from someone that can work with you like a therapist, friend, or family member.

## Step 2: Center yourself in the present while taking in slow and deep breaths

Once you know what trigger you would like to work on, it is essential that you pause for a moment and close your eyes. Take in slow and deep breaths for about 5-10 minutes. Breathe from your belly and allow your whole body to come to the point of relaxation.

Focus your mind on your breath with your eyes closed. In your mind, scan your body from head to toe, allowing every tension to be released. Let loose every tightness in your body so that you relax.

## Step 3: Identify and feel your emotions

While feeling centered in your breathing, start to bring that trigger into your mind. You can do this by simply trying to recall the latest/most recent occurrence. Avoid making any judgments and pause for a moment to get in touch with your feelings and sensations. Take note of any emotions and feelings you had inside.

Now, try to take deep and slow breaths while still feeling what you felt when you had the occurrence. Begin to ask yourself what you are feeling at that moment. Do you feel anger? Do you feel scared? Are you anxious? Start looking for the emotions that run beneath it. Anger is but a secondary emotion that comes on as a means of trying to protect yourself from feeling vulnerable.

Is there something that underlies that anger? Is it hurt, shame, fear, or something else? What emotional feelings do you have? Write them down on a plain sheet of paper or in a journal.

## Step 4: Feel and take note of the location of sensations in your body

At this point, it is critical that you take a moment, pause, and feel each emotion run through your body. Take note of the sensations that you feel at different parts of your body. For each of the emotions that are triggered, record the sensation that you feel and what part of the body you feel it in. You can do this by ensuring that you maintain the picture of your triggering event in your mind.

## Step 5: Accept your feelings and have the confidence that you can handle your emotions and sensations

Here, it is important that you keep reminding yourself that your emotions do not define who you are. You are not your emotions but just an observer of your emotions. Tell yourself that those emotions that you have are energy, and your feelings are pockets or charged energy that is associated directly with your past pains and wounds.

In other words, as a choice-maker for your life, you have the free-will to choose what you want. You can breathe into painful, fearful, and anxious situations. As you do that, notice those sensations, and emotional feelings shift, move away, and allow yourself to release them. Affirm to yourself that you have the power to accept these feelings as they are at that very moment.

Start telling yourself that you can handle it. Tell yourself that you are strong enough to handle the situation with ease, calm, and wisdom. Realize that one of the most powerful leverages that you have over negative emotions is reminding yourself about the time you had them and how you handled them successfully.

## Step 6: Identify what you tell yourself in your mind that triggers pain

Now, start taking note of your thoughts as you picture the triggering event. Record any toxic thoughts and feelings that come through your mind. The truth is, what you think often triggers an emotional feeling and physical sensations in your body. This is just how the brain functions.

All you have to do here is to watch those thoughts from afar. Remember that you are not the emotion or the thoughts; you are simply an observer that is taking note of things as they happen without making any judgments.

Whenever you get disturbing thoughts, imagine riding in a luxurious train that is speeding. Imagine that you are looking out the window taking note of every thought or emotion that causes anger and then quickly close the window as you get back to your comfortable seat, your safe place.

Record everything that you tell yourself while you have that self-talk adjacent to the emotions and physical sensations you experienced.

## Step 7: Empathetically connect so that you can understand and validate your experiences

It is important that you keep reminding yourself that even though other people or situations may trigger a painful feeling in you, they are not the cause of your pain. It is your self-talk that is causing you so much pain. It is what you tell yourself that is triggering the resentment, anger, guilt, and frustration, among other emotions you may be experiencing.

# Chapter 11.  Make a Change of Yourself

### Problem Solving

Cognitive-behavioral therapy's goal is not to tell yourself that everything is OK and that there are no problems. There are, for all of us. Rather, the aim is to achieve a balanced, realistic view of different situations that allows us to react effectively and without excessive fear, anxiety, or low mood. While thought and belief challenging are useful when thoughts and beliefs are not true or when a situation is unchangeable, problem-solving is good when a situation is changeable but may be fraught with anxiety. Problems may also be connected with depression, medical issues, addiction, or family issues. Some types of problems that could be addressed with this model include improving communication with your spouse, reducing your debt, dealing with a restriction imposed by illness, adhering to a new diet, quitting smoking, getting to work on time, figuring out child care, or reducing the severity of disease symptoms.

The problem-solving approach taught with CBT has seven steps.

**Step 1:** Identify and describe the problem. The first step is describing the problem in detail. Write down what it is, the time frame, who it involves, where it happens, and so on. If you think your description might be exaggerated, you can use some evidence-for-or-against techniques to assess it more accurately. Choose a specific problem that is likely to have a concrete solution.

**Step 2:** Identify possible solutions. Brainstorm all possible solutions you can think of. Don't worry about the details at first, since even a ridiculous-sounding solution can lead you to a more realistic one. Think about the advice you might give a friend in this situation, or what you've done in similar situations. You can also ask others for advice. Keep an open mind.

***Step 3****:* Evaluate possible solutions. Once you have a few possible solutions, write down the pros and cons of each one. In some cases, you may need professional advice from a doctor, lawyer, or administrator.

***Step 4****:* Decide on optimal and backup solutions. Based on the pros and cons of the possible solutions, decide on the best solution and one or two backup solutions. Alternatively, you can simply rank the solutions in order of preference.

***Step 5:*** Plan what you need to do. Plan out detailed steps needed to enact the solution you identified. Breaking it down into small steps can make it more approachable.

***Step 6:*** Carry out your plan. Do the steps you listed in Step 5. If needed, shift to one of your backup plans.

***Step 7:*** Check and adjust the plan as needed. How did it go? Is the problem solved or reduced to a manageable level? If the problem is not solved or if a new problem has arisen, you can return to Step 1 and formulate a new solution and plan.

### Sleep

There are things you can do in your life outside the CBT strategies that can greatly benefit your well-being and increase the effectiveness of any therapy you use. One of the most important factors is sleep. Enough sleep is important for mood, energy levels, physical health, and even the chemical balance of the brain. Things like anxiety can make it harder to sleep, creating a reinforcing cycle of stress and exhaustion.

However, you can make many simple changes to help yourself get a good night's sleep:

- Don't oversleep by more than an hour to make up for lost sleep.
- Don't watch TV, use electronics, or eat in bed.
- Give yourself thirty minutes to an hour before bed to relax.
- Avoid napping more than twenty minutes during the day if it makes it hard to sleep at night.
- Not everyone needs eight hours of sleep per night. Focus on getting restful sleep, rather than getting "enough" sleep, which can lead to more anxiety.
- Avoid caffeine, alcohol, and nicotine in the four hours before going to bed, or avoid them entirely if you find that you are sensitive to their effects.
- Get physical activity during the day, but not late in the evening.
- Ask your doctor about the side effects of medications—some can lead to trouble sleeping.

### Healthy Eating

Many people also find that a healthier diet contributes to a better sense of overall well-being. It can also contribute to weight loss and improvement of other health factors, relieving anxiety in the process. If you feel that addressing your diet now would lead to more anxiety, leave it for another time. However, if you feel motivated to improve your diet, go for it. It could be an effective way to feel healthier and less anxious or depressed.

The Mediterranean and DASH (Dietary Approaches to Stop Hypertension) are best supported in terms of scientific literature, and both can be delicious, flexible, and sustainable in the long term. Outside specific approaches, you can simply aim to eat more fruits, vegetables, whole grains, fish, healthy fats like olive oil and avocado, nuts, and seeds, and less red meat, high-fat dairy, white flour and refined grains, sugars, hydrogenated oils, and processed foods in general. If you enjoy cooking, taking cooking classes, and making healthier home-cooked meals could be a great part of your behavioral-activation strategy.

### Physical Activity

In behavioral activation, we mentioned physical activity as a way to improve mood. Physical activity does not have to mean exercise. Many people believe that they must go to the gym and run on a treadmill or ride a stationary bike for it to count. This is not at all true! There are many enjoyable ways to be active that don't take you anywhere near a gym. Walking, biking and hiking outside can be fun and relaxing, and research shows that a brisk walk can be just as helpful as a run for improving long-term health. Winter sports like skiing and skating are great too. Low-intensity activities like gardening, playing catch with your child, doing yard work, or actively cleaning the house count as well.

### Mantra Meditation

Meditation is a great way to relieve stress and cultivate mindfulness. There are many approaches, but one easy way to begin is mantra meditation. It is a form of meditation where one chooses a sound or phrase and repeats it anywhere from a few to hundreds of times. It can be as simple as a soothing sound, such as "om" or "ahh," or it can be a phrase in any language expressing sentiments of compassion, kindness, or peace. You can make one up yourself or use a traditional ancient mantra that has been murmured for centuries. There is great flexibility in mantra meditation, making this powerful technique all the more approachable.

It expresses a wish for well-being for all, peace for all, wholeness for all, and happiness for all. Again, you can find many videos online that can help you get the hang of chanting by searching for this phrase.

If none of these mantras resonate with you, or if you'd just like to make something more personal, you can create your mantra. It can be as simple as a sound—play around with making different "ahh," "eee," and "hmmm" sounds until you find one that feels soothing and calming. To create a compassionate mantra, first, think of the sentiment you want to express. It could be related to loving-kindness and acceptance toward yourself and others, wishes for peace, or anything else you want to remind yourself of. Then, try to find words that fit the meaning, which is easy and pleasant to say many times in a row. Work on paper if you find it helpful, or simply say the words aloud. Things like "love for all beings" or "peace within and without" could work. Once you've chosen a mantra, you can begin the meditation!

### Nature Therapy

Recent studies have found that interacting with nature regularly has a tremendous impact on our sense of health, happiness, and well-being. This is especially true for creative, rather than knowledge-based, interaction. You don't have to be working or trail running, just meandering along a path, sitting in a pretty clearing, or sketching something you find beautiful. One of the biggest impacts is on stress levels. In a 2014 study titled "The Influence of Urban Green Environments on Stress Relief Measures: A Field Experiment," researchers in Finland concluded that short visits to woodlands or urban parks measurably increased positive feelings and led participants to feel restored while decreasing stress and levels of cortisol.

### Nature

We've already talked about some of the benefits of being in nature for stress reduction. Nature is also a powerful source of awe-inspiring moments: experiencing beautiful sunsets, mountains, waterfalls, crashing waves, stunning coastlines, giant trees, and wondrous animal life can make you feel both small and wonderfully connected to the rest of the living world. Pondering the fact that the mountains you're standing on have been there for millions of years, that the tree towering above you is made up of tiny cells distantly related to your own, or that the birds stopping to rest in your backyard inherently know how to migrate thousands of miles can provide perspective and shift your focus away from aspects of your life that you perceive as negative.

Seek out these experiences as much as possible. If you have vacation time, make a point to go somewhere with natural beauty, whether it's on the other side of the world or just an hour away at a nature reserve. If you like adventure activities, do something exhilarating in a beautiful place, like skiing, mountain biking, paragliding, or windsurfing. Walking, hiking, cycling, horseback riding, or just relaxing in the presence of stunning natural features can help you experience a sense of awe and put things in perspective.

### Stargazing Therapy

You may enjoy Carl Sagan's famous "Pale Blue Dot" video—simply search for that title online, and several videos will come up. It is a wonderful meditation on the tininess of earth and humanity, both humbling and moving.

### Spirituality

Too often, spirituality gets overly muddled up with organized religion. These two are not the same thing. All humans have a spiritual capacity and inclination. It has nothing to do with stating certain beliefs, deferring to a man with a special outfit, or reading specific reading materials. Spirituality is our innate sense of wonder about our origins, our desire to question and ponder and reflect on the meaning of it all, and our ability and willingness to transcend the material world and our physical wants in search of something that feels more profound.

### Art and Music

The beauty and depth of human expression through art and music can be moving and awe-inspiring. Listen to singers whose voices you find truly unique and beautiful. Put on an opera or a symphony with a fabulous, sweeping finale. Look at paintings and sculptures that are stunning in their aesthetic, technique, or capture of emotion. Read poetry that touches you with its sincerity and creativity.

# Chapter 12. Break Toxic Connections

The reason why they seem so automatic in triggering all sorts of negative emotional responses is that you've made a habit of responding to them that way. You continuously pick out the worst interpretation. If you think about it, this makes a lot of sense on an abstract level because, just as with any system, we're always looking to make the most natural, most efficient connections. In other words, we're continually looking for the path of least resistance. Accordingly, our minds will always look at specific triggers and make the quickest connection because it takes too much effort to examine things based on the facts thoroughly

While this "efficient thinking" works out in many different settings, making routine decisions, for example, it comes to your mental associations; this can lead to a sense of powerlessness. It's effortless to feel that as long as certain situations pop up, your mind and emotions automatically go on autopilot, and you end up doing negative things. It's easy to conclude that there's not much you can do to break out of this cycle.

For example, it's one thing to say to yourself that you forgive your ex-girlfriend for breaking your heart. Still, the other time you see a friend of yours tag her name on social media, you get triggered. The tears come; the anger flashes. Whatever the case may be, the emotions are strong, and you are probably kicking yourself for feeling that way. However, this highlights the fact that there are some emotional habits you need to let go of.

## You Need to Break Toxic Connections on a Separate Track With Narrative Reform

Narrative reform, complete with inventory and disruption processes, is essential. However, you have to do that separately. It can take quite a while. For you to start feeling better in the here and now, as far as your automatic behavior and thinking patterns are concerned, you need to take steps now in breaking whatever toxic connections you suffer from.

Prepare for Situations

How exactly do you get off an emotional roller coaster when certain situations trigger a wave of negative emotions that could make you make bad choices? Just like swimming at the beach and dealing with waves, you can just randomly swim around and hope that a stream doesn't hit you or prepare for the coming waves. I hope it's very obvious to you, which is the smarter direction to take. It's much better to make for situations that trigger you than merely resolving to "steel" yourself the other time it happens.

Usually, when you intellectually think that you've broken apart your habits, and you know the right way to respond, things will fall apart once you're there. It's one thing to talk theory; it's another to live through an experience that involves all sorts of real-world triggers. This is why preparing for such stressful situations makes a lot more sense. Here's how you do it.

### Dress Rehearsal

Remember the last time you got triggered? Maybe somebody looked at you the wrong way. Or somebody said a word that made you feel bad? Whatever the case may be, repeat that scene in your head. List down the names, the looks that they gave you, and the full range of signals that you perceived negatively. Once you have that list of triggers, rehearse in your mind how you would respond. There are several ways you can deal with such triggers.

One, you can choose to reinterpret them. Maybe the person was just having a tough time and had that look on his or her face. Perhaps there was some sort of mix-up you weren't fully aware of, and that's why they were acting a certain way. In other words, it's all on them. It has nothing to do with you. When you choose to respond to a trigger that way, it's hard for you to find yourself in a negative emotional place because it's not about you. This is a powerful way of taking yourself out of the equation because the issue behind the signal remains entirely with the person sending that signal.

A great approach to this dress rehearsal is merely going over the different coping mechanisms and strategies you could take to judge another person. It's just a miscommunication on their part. They're having a tough time. Maybe they have issues. Perhaps they are confused. Whatever it is, it has nothing to do with you. You have to go through that mental list. Furthermore, you have to learn how to take specific factual details of what's happening around you and reinterpret them in such a way that leads to those conclusions.

Instead of instinctively balling up your fist and smacking that person in the head, you open your palm and reach out in collaboration. You choose to sidestep your typical reactions to something more proactive, collaborative, and it all might lead to a more positive ending. There are many ways you can do this. What's important is that you go through dress rehearsals. Don't just focus on the words being said. Focus on the visuals. Imagine yourself in a situation where this person says something or does something to you.

Keep going through these dress rehearsals, so when they do happen, you're not left with your essential default response. You're no longer restricted to merely reacting to what happens. Instead, you are responding based on your highest values. This is crucial because if you do not answer based on your highest values, you don't develop them. When you don't improve them, you don't incorporate them into your character. You do a lousy job of communicating with other people around you that you do have those high values.

The bottom line is simple: act to produce positive feedback. At the very least, act, so you provide neutral feedback. Believe me, and this is so much better than the negative feedback loop your automatic reactions routinely produce.

### Prepare Your Happy Place

Everybody has a happy place. This is not necessarily a geographic place or a location on a map. It can be a pleasant memory. Think back to when you were a kid, and your mom cradled you and lovingly smiled at you. You felt totally accepted, wholly protected, and loved. Imagine a scene where you had both of your parents, giving you all the attention, love, and care you could ever need.

This is a potent memory because you feel complete. There's nothing missing. There's no judgment. When you remember these scenes, you think there's nothing wrong with you. There's nothing for you to prove. Everything is where it should be. You feel at ease. You need to zero in on such memories and pay attention to the range of emotions they bring to the table. Most people have at least one happy memory. Call this your happy place.

When selecting a happy memory, make sure that you focus on the following: You must feel entirely accepted. It must give you a sense of total fulfillment. Nothing is missing in the scenario. There's nothing that you have to prove. You don't have to be somebody you're not. You don't have to impress people. You just are.

This comes handy when you're in a stressful situation. This is useful when you are around people who usually trigger you. Instead of simply resigning yourself to yet another wild and bumpy ride on that emotional roller coaster, you make it stop. How? You apply the brakes by merely calling or triggering your happy place. Just as you are stirred up by "negative stimuli," you can also counteract those triggers with your comfortable home.

Allow yourself to feel emotionally transported and relaxed. At the very least, when you think about your happy place, things aren't in crisis mode. You're not in a worst-case scenario. You have room to breathe. You have room to connect the dots and understand that there is a way out of the problem instead of continually getting your "fight or flight" processes triggered.

Adopt Physical Triggers for Your Happy Place

It's easy to think that your happy place ultimately has just to be a rational response. On paper, that sounds great. On paper, everybody is capable of a sensible answer to triggers. However, when all these negative emotions are flooding you, you really can't reach back quickly and find that comfortable spot and take refuge there. In many cases, it's too little too late. The better approach would be to adopt some sort of physical trigger.

One common way of triggering your happy place is to breathe deeply simply. When you breathe deeply and measure your breaths and close your eyes, it's easier to visualize that happy place. It's easier for you to benefit from the emotional relaxation and sense of completion, contentment, and serenity it brings to the table. There has to be some sort of physical trigger; otherwise, it's too easy just to bounce from one emotional signal to another and find yourself lost.

You also have to create a positive feedback loop using your happy place. For example, if you are caught in an argument, and somebody is close to cursing you out, you need to pull that happy place with a deep breath and then create a positive feedback loop by serenely smiling at them and then talking a bit slower to go calmly through the issues. This puts them at ease. At least they're not feeling that you are going to turn and fight them. At least it creates an opening for genuine dialogue. As you call and draw from the internal happy place you have, it becomes easier for you to smile or even joke in what would otherwise be a tense and possibly explosive situation.

### Change Positive Triggers

In addition to a happy place and the trigger for that response, you should also look for positive triggers. When you spot these, allow yourself to feel empowered, positive, and happy. Of course, these have to be contextual. They have to make sense in light of what else is going on. You would not want to find yourself in a funeral, for example, and be triggered by somebody smiling serenely at the deceased and allow yourself to feel ecstatic. That would not make any sense. It has to be contextual. Regardless, you need to do this. Find positive triggers in any situation that will allow you to feel empowered, positive, and happy.

## This Is All Good and Everything, but ... Now Comes the Hard Part

Let me tell you it's not going to happen overnight. We're all creatures of habit. As I mentioned earlier, we almost always instinctively take the path of least resistance. That's just how we're wired.

Accordingly, you have to keep at it. You have to prepare for your happy place. You have to defuse these negative signals in your head. You have to take the initiative. This takes a lot of energy.

However, the good news is that the more you do it, the more you get used to it. It becomes harder and harder for you just simply to react. Instead, you allow yourself to respond based on your best values. You're able to put on your best face. You're ready to bring out the best in you in what would otherwise be a very negative situation.

# Chapter 13. How to Practice CBT with your Everyday Life

### Low-level Physical Exercise

Low-level physical activity can offer some great benefits. I recommend that you use this type of exercise as much as you like, as long as your body is okay with it. These types of activities are least likely to worsen stress. Instead, they should feel very relaxing.

Low-level physical exercise can be a walk, a yoga session, a leisurely bike ride, a hike, or anything else that isn't very physically challenging. Doing low-level physical exercise every day can be perfect for your stress levels. It doesn't have to be that difficult. All you have to do is walk around for a bit (preferably in nature).

### Resistance Training

If you have the energy for it, doing some resistance training once in a while can be very good for your resilience to stress and overall health.

Resistance training is when your body pushes against a force. The most common types of resistance training are weight lifting and other types of strength training. It sounds stressful for the body to do some heavy weight lifting, you might think. And you would be entirely right. However, it is a bit more complicated than that.

Resistance training does put some stress on your body in the short term. This is not necessarily a bad thing if you have a proper routine, though. The key to appropriate training of resistance routine is enough recovery time. I recommend six to nine days. When you do resistance training this way, you will make your body momentarily stressed after the exercise.

However, when you allow your body to recover for six to nine days, it will increase your resilience to stress in the long term. So, when you follow this routine, you exchange some short-term stress for long-term stress relief and resistance.

However, if you're already much stressed, you might not want the temporary stress increase from resistance training. That's why I recommend that you only do resistance training if you feel like you have enough energy to do it. If you do, it can be very beneficial for you and make you more resilient to stress over time.

### Aerobic Exercise

Aerobic exercise is prevalent, and it can be beneficial. However, it can also require a lot of effort and time, which can be quite stressful.

Aerobic exercise, also known as endurance training or cardio, can be like running, swimming, or cycling. Or it can be almost any sports that require constant movement. If you have an existing practice of this type of exercise that you like, you can keep doing that. Especially if it also includes good social relationships - however, aerobic exercise is typically not the first type of activity that I would recommend for people with chronic stress issues. That's because endurance training is frequently seen as something you must do every day, or at least three to four times a week, for 30-60 minutes to get good results. This can be a lot of time for you to invest, which you don't have to. Plus, it can be very taxing for your body and just put more stress on it. You don't have to do aerobic exercise for several hours every week to see excellent benefits from your exercise routine.

Like I said, if you have an aerobic exercise that you like that makes you feel better, you can keep doing that. However, I would only do aerobic exercise several times a week for the fun it could provide, not necessarily for the benefits. If you have fun doing it, it can be significant. However, if you want the health benefits and better resilience to stress in a short time as possible, there are better ways.

### HIIT

High-intensity interval training (HIIT) gives you a combination of the sound effects of aerobic exercise and resistance training in a short amount of time. It improves your mitochondria; it helps with detoxification and weight loss and dramatically increases growth hormone levels. In other words, it is perhaps the best way to exercise for your health.

In a HIIT workout, you shift between doing high-intensity intervals and resting. For example, you can sprint for 60 seconds and then sit or lie down for 90 seconds. And when I say sprint, I mean race. You want to get some real effort into those 60 seconds, so your heart rate rises as much as possible. When your heart rate is high, you will get the benefits of aerobic exercise while relaxing between the intervals.

However, HIIT doesn't have to be running. It can be anything that allows you to do a high-intensity interval and get your heart rate quickly. The best thing about HIIT is that it takes very little time. You simply do the intervals for as long as you can, or for a maximum of 15 minutes in total. This means that you will, at most, be doing six sprints or other high-intense intervals.

Furthermore, you only have to do this once a week. Just once a week will give you amazing benefits. You don't have to put more time into it. When you combine HIIT with low-level physical activity throughout the week, your exercise routine will require almost no time, and it will have many benefits. Your resilience to stress should also increase significantly.

### Nutrition

What one eats directly impacts the way he/she feels? Aim to eat a balanced diet made up of low-fat proteins, fruits, vegetables, and complex carbohydrates. Lessen your consumption of foods that may negatively affect your mood or brain, such as alcohol, caffeine, saturated fats, and foods that have high chemical preservatives level or hormones.

Do not skip your meals. Aim to eat something at least every 3 to 4 hours since going for an extended period between your meals might make you feel tired and irritable.

Minimize refined carbs and sugar. You may desire or have a craving for baked goods, sugary snacks, or comfort foods like French fries or pasta, but these foods quickly cause lower energy levels and a crash in the mood.

Concentrate on complex carbohydrates. Increase your intake of foods, such as whole-wheat pasta, baked potatoes, whole-grain bread, and oatmeal as they can enhance serotonin levels without causing a crash. Increase your vitamin intake; eat more leafy greens, citrus fruit, eggs, chicken, and beans. Eat superfoods, like spinach, brown rice, and bananas, are rich in boosting mood.

Omega-3 fatty acids can also play a vital role in steadying and stabilizing one's mood. Some of the best sources are oily fish, salmon, mackerel, anchovies, sardines, and herring.

When preparing fish, you should bake or grill rather than fry them.

## Meditation

I was skeptical about meditation at first, but once I started utilizing it in my everyday routine, that skepticism quickly faded. It has been one of my favorite methods of removing negative emotions from my life and recovering with a nice dose of positive emotions and spirituality.

Meditation works to rejuvenate your mind, which makes it much more resilient when negativity does arise in your life. It not only rids us of all those harmful chemicals, stress, and anxiety in a physical way but in an emotional sense as well.

Be Thankful

Gratitude, no matter in what context, always has the power to instill more happiness in our lives. Scientifically, it gives our brains a big dose of dopamine, which is a 'feel-good' chemical that erases negative emotions and thoughts.

Mindfulness training

Mindfulness meditation or mindfulness training isn't explicitly a device for cognitive restructuring; however, it's an extraordinary method to prepare yourself to be careful (mindful) of your thoughts when you find yourself lost in them. General awareness of thinking is a fundamental first step in controlling your mind.

Mindfulness training includes picking a focal point of attention like breathing. For a set number of minutes, you center on experiencing the simple act of breathing to focus your mind. One of the most accessible breathing techniques to practice is the relaxation breathing, also known as square breathing. Here is how to go about it:

**Step 1:** Get yourself a quiet spot where you can sit still for ten to fifteen minutes without distractions.

***Step 2:*** Take note of your usual breathing pattern and check how long each inhales and exhales take.

***Step 3:*** Once you have pattern estimation, increment the length of the inward breath and exhalation by one second, basically hindering each inhales and exhale. When you have adjusted to the new, slower rate, add another second to each inhalation and exhalation. If you feel awkward or winded, it likely means you are slowing down too quickly. Proceed with continuously slowing your breath until you are breathing as slowly as you can with no trouble.

***Step 4:*** Once you are settled with a much slower breath, explore by holding after every exhalation and inhalation. These delays can be short, for a couple of seconds, or long, for as long as ten seconds. However long the pauses endure, note that you will likely need to alter your exhalation and inhalation pace to keep breathing without strain, without wanting to pant for air. The strategy is called square breathing because initially, the inhale, the exhale, and the two delays were intended to be of the same length. Similarly, each side of a square is of equal measure. Be that as it may, it doesn't generally make a difference, as long as fewer breaths are taken every minute.

***Step 5:*** Set an alarm and proceed with this exercise for ten to fifteen minutes. You will, in all likelihood, experience and increment in relaxation, and a considerable decline in angst.

The square breathing strategy works similarly as the smile strategy: Normally, when we are tense, our body reacts by increasing the breathing rate, and we take shorter, shallower breaths. When we are calm, the inverse occurs. By slowing down the breath, we stunt our minds into thinking we are relaxed, and most of the relaxing neuro-synthetic compounds are discharged. Research has indicated that taking part in this strategy has a quick impact on the brain. More significantly, studies have shown that participating in square breathing twice a day has a constant lower level of anxiety in people who are inclined to stress.

At whatever point, any anxiety- triggering thoughts come into your brain, slowly (and without self- criticism) take your mind back to experiencing the awareness of your breathing.

# Chapter 14.   Develop a Positive Mindset

The study of the internal mental processes of everything that goes on in your mind and influences it is called cognitive psychology. In every human brain, there is perception, thought, attention, memory, problem-solving, learning, and language.

Cognitive-behavioral therapy focuses on transforming a patient's behavior by understanding how their brain works and changing their thoughts. In essence, therapists are usually focused on turning a person's mindset from a negative one to a positive one.

Perhaps it would be easier for someone to understand how difficult it is to transform one's behavior by comparing it to anyone that has made a new year's resolution. Most of these resolutions get broken in a few weeks, and some never take off at all. The reason for this is the mindset.

CBT seeks to help a patient make lasting changes to their behavior. It involves investing in the time, emotions, and effort. According to psychologists, to create a permanent change in one's behavior, the individual must be willing to transform his or her mind.

## How to Start Changing Your Behavior

Probably you want to stop substance abuse, stop smoking, get rid of your eating disorder, or stop procrastination; no one solution works for all. Through a therapist, a person can try different techniques to achieve their goals.

Cognitive-behavioral therapy professionals use various techniques and focus on the goal they set at the beginning with the patient. During the process of therapy, a patient can get discouraged and give up on trying changing their behavior. On realizing this, a therapist must come up with ways to keep the patient motivated and focused.

Although change is not easy, psychologists have come up with various effective ways to help individuals transform their behavior. Researchers have also developed theories that aim at explaining how change occurs.

If a person wants to transform their behavior, getting to understand change elements, various stages of change, and how to work through each step, will help them achieve their goals.

### The Elements of Change

To succeed in changing one's behavior, and one needs to understand the most critical elements in behavior change. These are:

- Willingness to change – ensure you equip yourself with the knowledge and resources to make a successful, lasting change
- Obstacles to change – what things act as a barrier to your transformation
- Expect Relapse – what triggers can make you go back to your behavior

### Stages of Change

One of the most popular approaches to transformation is the Transtheoretical or stages of change model that researchers introduced to help people quit smoking. Studies have shown that the step of change model is instrumental in understanding how an individual goes through behavioral change.

Just as if cognitive behavioral therapy is gradual, change under this model is gradual too. The model recognizes Relapse as an unavoidable part of a long-term change process. Most people during the initial stages, resistors are unwilling to change. Still, with time, they develop an enthusiastic and proactive approach to behavioral change.

The change model stage illustrates that change is difficult and requires a gradual and systematic progression of small beginner steps towards a larger goal.

### Stage 1: Pre-contemplation

This is the first stage to change. During this initial stage, individuals do not consider a change and are described as being in denial. They believe there is no problem with their behavior. Ignorance of the problem and denial are what characterize this initial stage.

Some individuals in this initial stage feel resigned to their current state and believe they have no control over their behavior. They do not understand the damage of their behavior or are misinformed about the consequences of the behavior. If you find yourself in this stage, begin by evaluating yourself by asking questions like:

- If you have ever in the past tried to change the behavior,
- How would you realize you have a problem and
- What needs to happen for you to consider your behavior a problem?
- At this stage, a therapist will:
- Encourage the individual to re-evaluate their behavior
- Explain the risk of continuing with the said behavior
- Encourage self-reflection and introspection.

## Stage 2: Contemplation

During this stage, individuals become more aware of the benefits of making a change while at the same time, the cost of the replacement is more evident. The conflict between the interests and the cost of change can cause stagnation. The uncertainty at the contemplation stage can last for months and, in some cases, for years. Not many people make it past this stage.

This stage is characterized by ambivalence and conflicted emotions. An individual may view change as a process of giving up something instead of acquiring emotional, physical, and mental benefits.

If a person is contemplating a change in behavior, the person needs to ask themselves the following:

- Why do they need the change?
- What obstacles could be hindering them from changing?
- What can things help make the transition more manageable?

A therapist helping a person at this stage may do the following to help:

- Encourage the individual to consider the pros and cons of behavior change
- Help them confirm they are ready to change and encourage them through boosting their confidence in their abilities
- Help them identify the obstacles to achieving change.

### Stage 3: Preparation

During the preparation stage, an individual begins to make small transformations to prepare for more significant changes. For instance, if stop-taking alcohol is your goal, you may decide to reduce the quantity you consume. This will help reduce the alcohol content in your body.

An individual may also consider taking therapy more seriously or start reading self-helping reading materials. To improve the chances of making a lasting change, an individual is encouraged to take specific steps.

These may include:

- Gathering information on how to change one's behavior
- Come up with a list of statements that are motivating and draft your goals
- Identify an external resource like a support group such as Alcoholics Anonymous group near you.
- Associate yourself with friends or counselors that offer support.
- At this stage, a few strategies that would help include:
- Preparing an action plan
- Developing and writing down your goals
- Come up with a list of statements that motivate you.

### Stage 4: Action

At the fourth stage, individuals start taking action directly to accomplish their goals. The reason why many resolutions fail is that individuals do not stop to give much thought to the three stages.

If you make a resolution and jump from the initial stage to the fourth stage, changes are you will give up sooner than you thought. If you have decided to make changes, reward, and congratulate yourself for the positive changes, you take.

During this stage, ensure you get reinforcement and encouragement for every step because they help maintain positivity towards change. Check your motivations often, your progress, and resources, so you refresh your commitment and boost confidence in your abilities.

### Stage 5: Maintenance

This stage involves keeping away from past behaviors and their triggers and maintaining new practices. At this stage, an individual is more certain they retain their change, encouraging them to keep going.

To maintain the newly acquired behavior, you must identify ways to avoid temptations. Replace your old habits with new and positive ones. If you successfully can avoid Relapse, reward yourself, but should you Relapse, encourage yourself, and keep moving.

To be successful at this stage, an individual needs to:

1. Come up with ideal coping strategies for dealing with temptations
2. Motivate yourself by rewarding yourself for success

### Stage 6: Relapse

When a person is going through behavioral change, relapses are commonplace. When an individual goes through a decline, they will feel discouraged, frustrated, and disappointed. For success, a person should not allow the setbacks to undermine their self-confidence.

If an individual relapse, it is essential to take a moment, analyze what could have been the cause of the Relapse. Once you have identified the triggers, formulate a way to avoid the same triggers in the future.

Evaluate the techniques used, resources, and environment. Come up with a new plan of action that will commit you to your goals as well as how to overcome temptations in the future.

It is essential to know that relapses do occur at this stage, and you should not dwell on them, instead of formulating an action plan for the future.

### Change How You Process Information

Learning new habits is difficult for some people and a breeze for others. However, with the right mindset, one can do it. It is all a matter of determination and believing it is possible.

Researchers say that the brain is like plastic. It can allow change because it is static. As you go along life, your mind is modified. The experiences we go through help the brain to grow or to die. As you focus on change, it is essential to understand that the brain is not hardwired but flexible.

Your brain controls all your body functions, from how our organs function to how we behave and live within our environment. It is essential to control the central unit of the human being, which is the brain.

Your brain has two distinct parts, called the hemispheres. The right and left hemispheres of the mind focus on different things. If you find yourself focusing on the big picture, then you are using the right region of your brain. To focus on linear and more detailed information, the left hemisphere is in use.

When learning new skills or routines, you will use the right hemisphere. Once the methods become a habit, they are transferred to the left hemisphere. The brain has billions of neurons that are used to transmit information to other parts of the body. Neurons are continuously produced, making it possible for an individual to learn new skills at any age. This is what helps to make change possible.

# Chapter 15.   Identify Your Goals

It's essential to have goals in life. Goals are what give you direction. If you don't have goals, then you'll have nothing to work toward. However, taking a few moments to reflect on yourself and set some goals can help make considerable changes in your life. In general, it's essential to reflect on yourself regularly. You must acknowledge where you are and where you're headed. By setting goals, you are setting yourself up for success and have a plan for yourself. It will give you more motivation, as you will be working towards something that you genuinely value. It can help you to feel more confident about yourself. When you can identify what you want to improve and take steps to work on those, you will feel better about yourself. You'll see that it's possible to achieve whatever you put your mind to. To identify your goals related to mental health, you must first determine what issues you struggle with. This could be something that you know of, or you may have individual signs here and there. You may even simply wish to change your mindset and be more positive. Then, you must figure out how you're going to resolve your issues. Then, you may consider how you want to change your life. This could include adding habits, routines, and exercises for yourself. Then, you must bring all that knowledge together and learn how to set goals and stick to them.

### Identify Changes to Make

When starting to plan your goals, it's essential to identify what changes you would like to make. Do you want to think differently? Is there a particularly bad habit of yours that you would like to change? Consider what you want to change about yourself, and you'll be ready to take the other step. You may wish to change your mindset; you could want to focus more, you may decide that there is something that you struggle with, or you might want to take better care of your mental health. Regardless of what you want to change, it's essential to identify what you want. There are many aspects of yourself that you can improve.

You may want to work on your relationship with yourself. Perhaps you have a negative view of yourself. You may lack self-confidence and think of yourself as incapable of accomplishing what you want to. Maybe you are too hard on yourself and find it difficult to forgive yourself when you make a mistake. You may struggle with negative self-talk and find yourself bringing yourself down always instead of believing in yourself and feeling capable. It's also possible that you just need to work on being able to love yourself and be completely happy with yourself. Perhaps it's hard for you to be alone, but you want to work on appreciating your alone time and independence.

Perhaps you wish to work on your relationship with others. You may receive more than you give and work on being kinder to others. Maybe your relations are strained, or you have a particular relationship that you want to work on. You may want to start listening to others more instead of just waiting for your turn to speak. Perhaps you want to spend time with others more often. You may want to practice more random acts of kindness for others. Maybe you want to form deeper relationships with others and work on your dependability. You may even want to lower your expectations of others or be more understanding of others.

You might want to improve your ability to focus or your productivity. Maybe at work, you aren't able to focus on your work. This could be for several reasons. Perhaps you feel distracted by something that's bothering you, or you give in to procrastination. Maybe you multitask and find it hard to focus on one thing at once. You may also find it hard to keep your focus for an extended period. Or, you might want to get more done every day. You might spend more time taking breaks than you want to.

Perhaps you want to spend more time on your mental health. You may have an issue that you're aware of and want to fix. Maybe you need to get therapy. Or, you may not know what your problem is, and you'd like to find out. Perhaps you just want to spend more time taking care of yourself. You could wish to spend time relaxing, meditating, or doing what you love. Maybe you want to focus on improving your physical health so that your mental health also improves. You may want to educate yourself in many ways, and it's essential to set goals so that you can work toward making yourself better.

### Resolving Your Issues

Now that you know what you need to change, it's time to make a plan for changing your life. You must decide what you want to do to improve the areas that you want to make changes in. This could be changed in your lifestyle, changes in how you think, or habits that add-in. You may also want to seek help from a therapist. There are many ways to resolve your issues. Recognizing your problems is a first step in the right direction, but you must follow through with your goals to make changes.

You may first want to make changes in your lifestyle. If your goal is to improve your relationship with yourself, you may want to make moves toward spending more time by yourself doing what you love. If your goal is to improve your relationship with others, you might want to schedule more time with them. If you want to improve your productivity, you may begin to plan your time better. If you wish to improve your mental health, you may take time to work on it and seek the help of a therapist or do it yourself.

You may also want to alter the way you think. If you want to improve your relationship with yourself, you may begin by thinking more positively about yourself. To improve your relationship with others, you can start with compassion and understanding. Expressing these toward others can make a massive difference in the way you see them. To become more productive, you can start working on how well you focus and begin to see work differently. For improving your mental health, you may simply want to think more positively and become more aware of your thoughts and actions.

Adding in habits can help you to improve your life. They are often quite simple, yet have a significant impact on your life and happiness. You may add patterns that only take a few minutes a day to practice, yet they can completely change your way of living. By only taking time to yourself to relax or learn how to focus, you can build skills that you had no experience in. Further, taking time to yourself can also make you happier and more aware of your worth.

Getting help from a therapist is always a great option, as well. Because they are a professional in their field, they will be able to offer you the best advice and help you to feel better. They may help you feel less alone and can provide solutions to your problems that you may not have even considered. This is a wise option, especially if you have not been able to make changes on your own. A therapist will also be able to offer you an outside opinion on you.

## Making Changes

It's quite simple to start changing your way of living and implementing exercises into your daily routine. You may even do so without any costs or having to go anywhere. Improving your mental health and life as a whole can be accomplished by incorporating some daily habits and exercises into your day. Doing so is a great way to form a better relationship with yourself and feel happier. Your mental health will improve, and you'll be able to extend your positivity to others by creating a better relationship. You'll be able to concentrate better and get more done. Although therapy is always recommended, it may not be as necessary as it was before if you can help yourself to feel better. There are a few simple exercises that you can add to your daily life to help you to feel better and have a better day.

One great exercise is to take deep breaths. You can do this alone, or you can choose to start meditating. Either way, you will feel much better. You may relax and focus your attention. It's also a great way to take a step back from anything that is making you feel stressed or anxious. Taking just a few minutes to do so can help you. If you are at a desk all day, you may also choose to stand and stretch. Instead of staying seated all day, it's helpful to get up for a moment and move around a bit. This can keep you feeling awake.

It can be healthy to make time to interact with others. Make sure that you surround yourself with people who make you feel good. Ideally, you may spend time with people that make you happy and even laugh. This can boost your mood and help you to feel more satisfied. It's just as important, though, to spend time with yourself. Learn to appreciate time alone and recognize the difference between being alone and feeling lonely. You should become comfortable with yourself, as you will be there everywhere you go. You may want a quiet hobby that you can spend time doing, such as reading, running, listening to music, or knitting. These are great ways to get some time for yourself to do something that you enjoy.

You may also incorporate physical exercise into your routine. Yoga can be a great way to relax and relieve your stress. Cycling and running can be great ways to get outside and enjoy nature while moving around. There are many classes that you can take; you can get a gym membership or try at-home workouts. Whatever way works for you is the best. It doesn't matter how you exercise. What matters is that you enjoy it. Plus, you can even meet others like yourself that also enjoy what you do. This can be a great way to make new friends while doing something you love and exercising. It can also give you something to focus on, and you'll feel better about yourself.

# Conclusion

There is a common saying that health is wealth, and while this is the case, it is also indicative that mental health is wealth. The most common ailment that we have in the world that we live in today is the one that is affiliated to mental health, and this is tagged as the killer disease because of the way that it shrinks one into a state of the sickness.

Another factor that necessitated the stay of CBT is suicide. The rise of suicide over the years has been declared alarming. The American Psychological Association has stated that one of the killer ailments in the world is a suicide. This is so because people seldom talk about those areas of their mental health that is giving them problems. The CBT came as some sort of therapy to make such people feel the need to talk about what bothers them, intending to find a solution to those problems.

Much research was conducted on most of the mental health issues related in this. It has been discovered that if they are not well managed and taken care of, they are likely to cause death, and this is about the same thing that suicide causes. It should be noted that many of the mental health issues that are highlighted in this reading are such that they could lead to the thoughts of suicide if not well managed, and this is why people need to start thinking twice about the benefits of CBT as a medium of living a better life.

Many people have asked questions as regards how it is that they can overcome their mental health trauma. A lot of people have a mental health problem, but they are scared that they would be labeled if they have to come clean to a therapist and let him or her help them. There is a heightened amount of suicide cases every year, and depression itself is not growing at a rescind.

As we speak, in the United States of America, one of the hugest killers of human lives is affiliated with the mental health, and this is the reason why a lot of people need further sensitization on the topic because you do not know who might be going through the other trauma.

Traumas are a part of the human life there is no way that our lives would be complete. If at some point in time we do not experience some kind of trauma. But being that as it may, we owe ourselves a duty to be able to carry on our lives regardless of what kind of trauma we might be facing. This is why we have Cognitive Behavior Therapy and all of its processes to help with our mental health.

The first thing that we all have to let go of is what people think about us. If you have a mental health problem that you would love a therapist to help you with, you have taken the first make step towards having a better life. You are a lot better than one person who is standing amid the crowd and having a suicidal or depressive thought.

When you finally go for the CBT therapy, it is advisable to be cautious with your time by setting goals and outlining how early you want to round up the entire program. You are a lot better than you used to be.

Based on the situation and approaches that are defined as cognitive therapy or cognitive-behavioral therapy, the presence and relevance of the behavioral adjective also partly reflect the weight given to principles and procedures of direct behavioral derivation.

What unites all approaches that recognize the definition of cognitive therapy is the common emphasis on meaning structures and information processing and, therefore, the cognitive variable's recognition as the predominant explanation of the clinical phenomena. Furthermore, regardless of differences in procedures, the treatment method always involves the manipulation of the cognitive variable as the main tool for change.

Nigel still working on marriage
17 June 2018th. From 2016?
2017 Aug & October May 2018 First
4 August 2017.
Guy talking 28 June Rob wed (Michelle) 2019
at Kims Antonio
Wedding 3 months / March 5 months July first 2019
Say hung (Sep 2019).
at 6 month 10 days. 2 Turkish -7)
Nov.
21 October 219
6th month
No Antonio
But messaged Antonio october 2019
a few times 16 nov 2019
March April and sent
Picture Covid 1st 6th 7th
Jan 2020. Feb, October 2020
month?
Mo
Say 60%. Antonio Feb Covid Talk
Talk to Nigel August 6th month
about covid
messages
April May
never saw January
him (Proof)

(Honest)

Pee
Toilet
Flush
Door / Stairs
Check my phone  OK
Trying Tutor  Try the phone
Hello White  check my phone
Have you seen it
O my god
can you hear it
check
she will hear it